Seven Long Times

❖

Piri Thomas

Arte Público Press
Houston, Texas
1994

This volume is made possible through grants from the National Endowment for the Arts (a federal agency), the Lila Wallace-Reader's Digest Fund and the Andrew W. Mellon Foundation.

Recovering the past, creating the future

Arte Público Press
University of Houston
Houston, Texas 77204-2090

Cover design by Cindy Guire

Thomas, Piri 1928-
    Seven long times / by Piri Thomas
        p.   cm.
ISBN 1-55885-105-4
    1. Thomas, Piri, 1928- . 2. Prisoners-United States-Biography.
I. Title. II. Title: 7 long times.
HV9468.T55   1994
365'.4'092--dc20   94-8661
                                                         CIP

The paper used in this publication meets the requirements of the American-National Standard for Permanence of Paper for Printed Library Materials Z39.48-1984. ⊚

———————— ❖ ————————

To Joseph and Paula Gross, Betty,
Michael, Laura, and David,

to all those inside and outside
the prisons who know what is happening
and are doing something about it,

and as always
to my own Mom Dolores Thomas Montanez.
*Sorry she didn't live to see me turning out all
right.*

CONTENTS

ACKNOWLEDGEMENTS

Thanks to Leon King, my editor, whose patience and perseverance made this book possible; to Ossie Davis, for his long-time encouragement; to John Oliver Killens, whose book *Youngblood* spurred me to write; to Dr. Evelina Antonetty (Tati), for her love throughout the years; to Mama Bishop, a second mother to a lot of us; to José García, a beautiful brother from way back; to Elva, Tony, Tony, Jr., and Paulie; and to Phyllis LeBeau, Humberto Cintrón, Lou Delemos, Jay Harris, Hannah Weinstein, Allison Vogel, Pam, Maggie (Floating Foundation of Photography), Bobby García, Herman Badillo, Bella Abzug, and Louis Negron.

Up and down I look all around
I'm stuck in this square block of mind

Here and there—I look everywhere
I'm stuck in this square block of mind

Straight and away—there must be a day
That I'll be free from this square block of mine.

Seven Long Times

PROLOGUE

Like I'm standing here and nuttin's happening. Diggit, man, what's in this here world for me? Except I gotta give, give, give. I'm tired of being a half-past nuttin'. I've come into this stone world of streets with all its living, laughing, crying, and dying. A world full of backyards, rooftops, and street sets, all kinds of people and acts, of hustles, rackets, and eye-dropper drugs. A world of those who is and those who ain't. A world of name-calling, like "nigger sticks" and "*mucho* spics."

I'm looking at me and no matter how I set my face, rock-hard or sullen-soft, I still feel the me inside rumbling low and crazy-like, like I'm mad at something and don't know what it is. Damn it, it's the craps of living every day afraid and not diggin' what's in tomorrow. What's the good of living in a present that's got no future, no nuttin', unless I make something. I fell into this life without no say and I'll be a mother-jumper if I live it without having nuttin' to say.

I know this world is on a hustle stick and everybody's out to make a buck. This I can dig, 'cause it's the same here on the street. I gotta hustle, too, and the only way to make it is on a hard kick. I dig that—copping is the main bit and having is the main rep. You see, I'm really trying to understand and see where you're at.

How many times have I stood on my street corner, looking out at your blippy world full of pros? At all you people who made it and got to be great, a real bunch of killer-dillers. I know about you. I've gone to the big school, too. I've dug how to live, too.

Are you willing to learn about me and what makes me click? Well, let me run it to you nice and easy.

Have you ever sensed the coming danger as on a bop you go? A rumbling of bravery, of *puro corazón*, and gusto to the *n*th degree? Have you ever punched a guy in the mouth with a ripped-off garbage can handle, or spit blood from jammed-up lips? Have you ever felt the pain from a kick in the balls? Have you ever chased in victory in a gang fight supreme or run in tasteless defeat with all the heart you can muster? Have you felt the bond of belonging when with your boys you went down?

Tell me, did you ever make out in dark hallways with wet kisses and fumbling hands? Did you ever smother a frightened girl's rejections and force a love from her? Did you fill your dreams with the magic of what you wanted to be only to curse the bitchin' mornings for dragging you back on the scene? Did you ever smoke the blast of reefers and lose your freakin' mind? Did you ever worry about anything at all—like a feeling of not belonging? Did you ever lover-dubber past this way?

Did you ever stand on street corners and look the other way from the world of *muchos ricos* and think, *I ain't got a damn?*

Did you ever count the pieces of garbage that flowed down dirty gutters, or dig the backyards that in their glory were a garbage dump's dream? Did you ever stand on rooftops and watch nighttime cover the bad below? Did you ever put your hand round your throat and feel your pulse beat say, *I do belong and there's not gonna be nobody can tell me I'm wrong?*

Say, did you ever mess with the hard stuff—that cocaine, heroin? Have you ever filled your nose with the wild kick coke brought or pushed a needle full of the other poison and felt the sharp-dull burning as it ate away your brain? Did you ever feel the down-gone-high as the drug took effect? And feel all your yearnings become sleepy memories and reality become illusion—and you are what you wanted to be?

Did you ever stand, small and a little quiet-like, and dig your mom's and pop's fight for lack of money to push off the abundance of wants? Did you ever stand with outstretched hands and cop a plea from life and watch your mom's pride on bended knees ask a welfare investigator for the needed welfare check while you stood there getting from nothing and resenting it just the same? Did you ever feel the thunder of being thrown out for lack of money to pay the rent, or walk in scared darkness—the light bill unpaid—or cook on canned heat for a bunch of hungry kids—no gas—unpaid?

Did you ever sneak into the movies and dig a crazy set where everybody's made it on that wide wild screen? They ride in long, down shorts, like T-Birds, Continentals, Caddies. Such *viva* smoothies, with the vines—the clothes—like you never ever saw. And, oh, man, did you ever then go out of that world to sit on hard stoops and feel such cool hate and ask yourself, "Why, man? Why does this gotta be for me?"

Have you ever known the coldness of getting busted...the scared, hollow feeling of loneliness as you're flung into a prison cell?

Have you ever heard voices inside you screaming, *Don't bitch about being busted, turkey—you done broke the law and that's wrong,* and had that truth eased off by another voice saying, *Don't fret, little brother. How could you ever have done it right when everything out there in them streets was so goddamn wrong?*

So carry the burden with *mucho corazón* and try like hell to make the shadows of the prison bars go away by closing your eyes to the weight of time.

Hard days, long nights. Without a name, a number instead. Your love of color blighted by a sea of monotonous blues and grays. Warmth replaced by cold steel bars. Tiny, bleak cells surrounded by chilly, concrete, mountain-high prison walls. Within is lost the innocence of a smile.... The tears that flow are unsalted and the laughter is unreal. The days that eventually turn into long years are each terrible in themselves;

You don't want to hear me. I'll make you hear me.
You don't want to see me. I'll make you see me.

BUSTED, LIKE GAME TIME!

Why in hell did this stickup have to be different from the others? Usually everything went smoothly, the modus operandi always being the same every time we stuck up a bar or cocktail lounge. Sometimes there would be three of us, sometimes four. We'd come into the place separately and set up strategic points. We'd order beers and would sip quietly while sizing up the place. When we were sure the spot was worth taking because of a minimum of danger from anything that looked like cops out of uniform, we'd look at each other and signal for the stickup to begin by wiping our fingerprints from our glasses of beer by running the sides of our fingers up and down all around the glass. The others would then get up and announce: "All right, everybody. This is a stickup. Just be quiet and nobody will get hurt—otherwise...?" And the guns in their hands made any further explanation unnecessary. One of them would herd all the customers against the wall while the other attended to the bartender or manager. I'd remain sitting, my position always being near the entrance.

Nobody got out and anybody coming in was quietly invited by me and the gun in my lap to come in and enjoy the get-together. I was twenty-two years old. My act was to be natural and give the appearance of quiet enjoyment. The cash and jewelry, meanwhile, were collected from everyone in sight. Then everybody would be herded into the bathroom and warned to be quiet. The jukebox or cigarette machine would be jammed up against the closed toilet door. The others would leave first while I covered them, and we'd all walk slowly to our car and drive away without suspicious haste.

There had been one stickup that hadn't gone so smoothly—the time we stuck up a bar-lounge near a railroad terminal. This time the customers were told to remain seated and continue their drinking because it wasn't three o'clock in the morning and we didn't have the safety edge of no people walking the streets. I sat at my usual place near the entrance. Feeling expansive as the stickup progressed, I asked the nervous bartender what was the best drink in the house.

"Courvoisier," he stammered.

I looked around at the frightened customers in the small but elegant lounge and told the bartender, "Fine, would you please serve Courvoisier to the ladies and gentlemen. It's on me."

The drinks were served and I watched some drink theirs at one gulp while others just sat there paralyzed from their scalps down. There were two hard-faced men sitting with two young women who looked like winners in a beauty contest. One of the men looked dead at me with no nervousness written on his face. I held the gun resting on my lap a little more firmly and stared back at him. He smiled and held up his glass of Courvoisier, toasting me, "Hey, kid. You sure are a cavalier."

The accent in his voice reminded me of the Italian cats from Pleasant Avenue over on the east side who were always driving around in big expensive cars and dealt in kilo-sized drugs. I smiled back and watched as he put his valuables in the paper bag being passed around by one of the guys. I said to no one in particular, "No wallets, please, just your cash and jewelry."

My attention kept going back to the hard-faced customers. My eyes took in their expensive clothes. *These cats sure look like Mafia, but fuck it—if they try anything, they can die, too.*

My partners finished their collection and were about to herd the customers into the john when all of a sudden the bartender bolted through an exit behind the bar and disappeared up a stairway, taking three and five steps at a time.

"Split, fellers," I yelled, still covering the customers, especially the hard-faced cats. My partners walked unhurriedly by me and headed for our car. "Nobody move, just sit there nice and easy, if you please." The one hard-face shook his head from side to side as if in amusement. I had the feeling he owned the joint. I backed out of the place, panning my German Luger over the scope of the lounge. I closed the door quickly and started walking fast, just short of running. My partners already had the car in motion. I turned my eyes back to the lounge and saw the bartender running out with a shotgun in his hands. I dove for the open door of our moving car, which suddenly took off at top speed and turned the corner just as we heard the explosion of the shotgun shells being blown our way. I held on to one of my partners, half of me hanging outside the car.

"Goddammit," I screamed. "Slow the fuck down so I can get in." The car didn't slow down, but I got in anyway, shaking from the sweats. I checked myself out to be sure I hadn't gotten hit.

"Close call," said one of the guys.

"Yeah, damn close," I said. "How'd the money look?"

"Pretty good," answered the driver. We slowed down to law-abiding speed and I counted over two thousand bucks and thought about the hard-faced cat who probably owned the joint. I wondered about his being a Mafia man and went back to counting and wondered no more.

There had been other jobs with narrow escapes...but this one now—this stickup fell apart. Half the police force in plainclothes seemed to be the only customers in the place.

It was a crazy feeling. Screams of people drowning in fear and the roar of gunfire filled the smallness of the nightclub. I peered through the murkiness of red and blue lights trying to see my two partners, but they were lost somewhere in the stampede of customers who were trying to duck cops' and robbers' bullets. I felt detached from the shit flying around

me. Part of me felt the fright of the customers, but I pressed
the trigger of my gun to fire at the bullets that were coming
at me from all directions. The bullets kept whizzing around
me like angry bees until one caught me somewhere in the
chest. Even if I had seen it coming, I don't think I would have
stepped aside, so unreal my being there seemed.

The bullet spun me around and stunned me with pain. I
felt the hot thick wetness of blood spreading all over my
chest. I squeezed the trigger, again sending bullets out there
at some blurred enemy who went crashing backward, sinking
into the same shadows I felt myself slipping into. Fighting
against unconsciousness, I shook my head clear and staggered in the darkness. I heard and dimly understood that my
shoes were slowly being filled with my own blood. The rest
was flashing police-car lights, wailing sirens, people staring,
and me inside an ambulance going at top speed.

Ceilings flashed by through a long corridor and hollow
voices sounded like echoes in a tunnel; I was in a world of
shadows peopled by uniformed policemen, doctors, and
nurses looming over me at random times. They looked unreal
in the haze of injections and whatever other preparations the
wounds to my abdomen were bringing to me. I closed my eyes
and listened to the buzzing in my head. My eardrums seemed
stopped up. I felt fingers touching, probing me. I opened my
eyes and saw the vague outline of a bottle of some red liquid
hovering by my side and felt a faint needle prick going somewhere into my arm. The roaring confusion melted from my
ears and I went down into a gentle dark, barely hearing
someone say, "Is he ready now?"

When I awoke, my mouth was dry with a taste of salty
blood, my chest was throbbing with an angry persistence. It
was difficult to breathe with two rubber lines shoved deep up
my nostrils. I lifted fingers heavy with weakness and felt my
chest. It was bound with miles of bandage. I opened my eyes
wider and saw a blur of people moving about, some in hospital white, some in policeman blue. Everything was like some
way-out nightmare that at times came together almost
clearly only to explode harshly in vivid recollection of stick-

ups, escapes, police sirens, more stickups, and a final stickup made of tissue paper that fell apart.

My mind reeled in a surge of recollections like a series of quick montages of the events that had led to my being there. From far off I heard a voice saying, "Yeah, he's awake," and a few seconds later I stared into the face of a policeman who was handcuffing my free wrist to the back of the bed.

He didn't speak to me. He just checked the handcuffs, stared at me for a second and went away. I looked around and saw many other patients in the large ward; it wasn't a prison ward because there were no bars on the windows and I was the only one handcuffed. I tugged at the handcuffs and the effort brought a loud grunt of pain that came tearing up from my insides. A nurse came and gave me an injection that eased the pain and sent me into a twilight world. My eyes closed of their own accord and my mind matter-of-factly thought, *Man, you're in trouble,* and began a chant of *escape—escape—escape—escape,* 'cause like, *coño,* man, anything or anyone trapped always thinks of escape. As the drug took whole effect, a part of my memory went back in time....

...Me and Ace Cruz, armed with two large pickle jars with tiny air holes punched in the top, had gone to Central Park to capture all the fireflies in existence. Hours later, we were sitting on the grass, our jars bursting with the eerie, cold green glow of dozens of fireflies.

"Wouldn't it be great if there was some way to put these bugs to work in our apartments? Free light, man."

"Not to mention light bulbs," added Ace.

"Shit, if those motherfuckers could give off heat, we could put Con Edison outta business."

"Good thinking, *bris.* Good thinking."

I dug my own fireflies and shook the jar upside down trying to dislodge them. But they cut right back to the tiny air holes.

"Diggit, Ace. They just stick to the top. Funny as hell."

"What's so damn funny?" he replied. "They're just trying to think how to fucking escape. Shit, wouldn't you?"

"Yeah." I turned the jar over and shook it. "You're fucking right I would."

We contemplated our imprisoned bugs in the evening light of Central Park and silently watched the on-and-off neon-like green glow.

"Piri." Ace's voice came through the semi-glowing darkness. "You think if these bugs hadda chance they'd do the same to us?"

I thought about it and said, "You fuckin' right. If I got treated this way, I'd get even. Like, we ain't got no right to stick 'em in a jar."

"*¿Por qué* we doing it then, *panín? ¿Por qué?*"

"'Cause we're stronger, chump. 'Cause we're smarter. That's why, moron." And I added softly, "'Cause we're meaner."

"You can't blame them for wanting to escape."

"No, you can't," I agreed.

Without checking with each other, we had silently opened our jars and with our fingers scraped free all them fireflies, which split every which way without so much as a nod of gratitude to us for letting them out. They could have at least spelled out in lights across the darkness of the Central Park sky: MUCHAS GRACIAS, FELLERS.

When I awoke again, it was evening. Pain was tearing up my insides. I had to protest somehow and swore out loud.

"Motherfucker...motherfucker." The words slamming loud and clear through the ward brought a mixture of snickering, outraged protest, misunderstanding, and sympathy from a rainbow of different ethnic voices.

The voice of a cop came up to my bed and suggested gently and without hypocritical kindness that I keep my goddamn black nigger mouth shut.

"You're going to be sent to Bellevue Prison Ward, you goddamn cop-shooting sonofabitch. If it was up to me, I'd send your black ass to the fucking morgue." The voice was saying all this to me in whispers only I was meant to hear. The voice went away mumbling, "All of you should be wiped off the face of the earth. Goddammit, if it was up to me..."

I fell asleep thinking of escape and wondering vaguely if whatever had me trapped in this jar would turn me loose as Ace Cruz and I had once done for a few dozen fireflies. *Honest to God, I'll light up the night sky with a blaze of me-lights:* GRACIAS, FELLERS.

As I was lifted onto a stretcher and put into an ambulance, in a dreamlike haze I tried to keep my gown together. Like everything was bad enough without having my bare brown ass out there for a free show. On a cold February day I was leaving St. Vincent's for Bellevue. In the street, with spots of snow grayly hanging on, I saw people looking at me, talking about me, handling me, and a vast sea of hostile cops. Finally, I turned the whole scene off and fell into a deep, friendly cushion of medicated sleep.

BELLEVUE PRISON WARD

Sunlight bounced off my eyelids and I opened my eyes
and tried to stare dead into the gleaming rays. I kept
my eyes open until they brimmed and burned with tears,
then closed them to the barred windows. Someone snatched
at my wrist and instinctively I jerked my hand away curled
in a fist.

"Take it easy, feller. Just checking to see if you're still
with us. You're a lucky kid." The doctor smiled.

"I ain't no kid, doc."

"Guess not. You people just seem to be born grown-up.
Feel much pain?"

"Damn right."

"Any trouble moving your bowels?"

"Yeah, it hurts to crap."

The doctor wrote something down on my bed chart.

"Beginning tomorrow, you start walking around."

"Are you kidding? It hurts just to fart."

"You want to heal all bent and twisted?"

I shook my head slowly from side to side.

"It's the best thing in the world for you, kid. When
women give birth, we get them up and around right away."

"I ain't giving birth," I snarled.

"The kind of mess you're in, you should be glad if you
were," he laughed. "I'll tell the nurse to give you something
for the gases." He jotted down something and walked away.

I looked around the ward and dug a lot of humanity in
pain, some moaning in bed, others moaning out of it. Practically all of them had on bandages like mine. Who knew
why—maybe bullet wounds, knife wounds, or maybe some

old lead pipes caving in part of their heads. Or just plain getting the shit kicked out of them in the police station.

I winced as I remembered the stickup and my own battle with the cops. The pounding from the red-faced Irish detective's fist against the side of my head was still vivid in my mind. I tried to stop thinking about all that had led to my being in Bellevue Prison Ward and to concentrate on the redheaded nurse who was leaning over to help another patient.

The nurse came to my bed, smiling. "Open up." Her green eyes twinkled. I opened my mouth and she popped a pill in it and handed me a glass of water. I swallowed the pill and smiled thanks.

"Open wide and lift your tongue."

"What for?"

"Just to make sure you swallowed your pill."

I smiled, recalling my long experience dealing in drugs out in the streets.

She leaned over and adjusted my bedclothes. Through the haze of rubbing alcohol surrounding her, my nose connected with a fragrance straight out of the Garden of Eden. It was pure woman. She caught me staring at her breasts. She didn't smile, but she didn't look mad. "I see you're getting well."

I watched her walk away. In the background I could hear voices arguing about a crooked whist game.

"You keep cheating and you ain't gonna live to stand trial."

"Motherfuck you, man. You're just bullshitting 'cause you're losing. If you can't pay, don't play."

I heard the faint thud of a fist slamming into somebody's face.

I eased the pillows about me and sat up. It was around noontime because the smell of food was overcoming the hospital odors of the ward. Attendants were giving out trays of food: meat, potatoes, vegetables, milk, and bread and butter. My mouth watered. An attendant set a tray in front of me, but it was the same food I had been getting—tea and soup. The redheaded nurse passed by and I called out.

"Hey, nurse, when am I getting some of that kind of food?"

"When the doctor says it's all right."

I ate, swallowing slowly, trying to make believe the tea and soup were *arroz con pollo*. When the tray was taken away, I killed time by listening to the sounds of the ward. People were moaning and groaning, arguing, getting medication, praying, and cursing. There were proclamations of innocence and the noise of bedpans being used. The smell of body sweat and antiseptics was strong. My eyes took in as much as I could see, but there were sections out of reach of my vision. I noticed four rooms across from me with heavy doors, each with a little look-see window cut into it. One door was slightly ajar; the space within was empty except for padding on the walls and doors. *Padded cells!*

There was a large toilet room, like one in Grand Central Station, as well as an office where a nurse sat looking at some papers, and an enclosed cubicle where a patient was talking to a civilian through a small screened opening. *Visiting room*, my mind noted. There was also a door marked EXIT guarded by a policeman. There were both male and female attendants...and the row of beds extended on either side of me.

I couldn't see any farther. I leaned back and took in the traffic of doctors and nurses, patients, attendants and porters, back and forth. I heard someone reciting and turned my head to see a tall, thin, cadaverous-looking white man of about forty-five years of age wearing a bathrobe and spouting Shakespeare to a theater audience only he could see. I listened to him awhile, his voice thin and rasping; he went from one thing to another..."To be or not to be"..."slings and arrows of outrageous fortune." My attention waned and I began to count the ward beds that were within sight, but stopped at nineteen because a warm West Indian voice broke into my isolation.

"Time for your temperature." The voice belonged to a chocolate-colored nurse of about forty.

"You're West Indian, aren't you?" I smiled.

"That's right, hon-nee. Kingston, Jamaica."

"Guessed right," I grinned.

"Feeling chipper, huh?" she singsonged.

"I should hope so. Well, let's have it."

She patted my leg and I eased painfully to my side and ignored the indignity of having that smooth sliver of glass expertly inserted. The nurse flipped the thermometer out and shook it furiously.

"What does it say?" I asked.

"That you're going to live. You ought to be thankful to sweet Jesus your light was not put out for you."

"Thanks a lot, Miss Belafonte." I made a wry face.

She laughed pretty-like. "My name is Mrs. Hylton, not Belafonte. Not that I would mind being Mrs. Harry Belafonte."

"Tsk, tsk," I joked. "What would your husband say to that kind of talk?"

"Not too much," she said gently, smiling. "He's been dead eight years."

"Mrs. Hylton, what's a favorite West Indian dish?" I changed the subject.

"Let me see. We have curry goat, lobster curry, nice and hot, and there is akee and codfish."

My tongue drowned in saliva, helplessly frustrated.

"Are you ready to start walking?"

Just the thought of it made me wince.

"Up you go." Nina Hylton was *mucho* strong. Perhaps it had something to do with curried goat and akee with codfish.

"Lucille," her voice twanged down the hall. The red-headed nurse came into view. "Please give me a hand. He's skin and bones but still heavy."

Each grasped one of my elbows and I began the creakiest, most painful walk in my whole freaking history. Everything in me seemed to be coming apart.

"Atta boy, champ. Glad to see you up and around." I recognized the voice of the accused cheater in the whist game of the night before.

"*Muchas gracias, amigo.*"

I looked at a thin, tall Puerto Rican of about twenty-five years with a Fu Manchu mustache and beard. He had light skin and hair like mine, unruly.

"Man, you in all the fuckin' papers. *Pistolas* and all that gangster shit."

"Aw, bullshit." I looked evil at him. He didn't seem to have any injuries.

"You don't look stabbed, shot, or blackjacked. You got some kind of disease?"

"Nay, man." He pulled at his long, thin mustache. "I'm here under observation. The court wants to know if I'm sane or insane."

"Are you?" I joked.

Fu Manchu's face grew serious. "If being sane is gonna get me a whole lot of time, and being nuts is gonna make it a short bit, then..." and Fu Manchu let out a blood-curdling laugh that made me raise my eyebrows. He could fool me anytime he wanted to play nuts. Smiling, he said softly to no one in particular, "The name of the game is sane or insane."

The walking exercises went on for a few days and then I was on my own. For a graduation diploma on my solo, Mrs. Nina Hylton handed me an enema, pointed to the john, and told me to take care of business.

In the bathroom I caught my reflection in the mirror. *My God, I look like something out of a concentration camp.* Man, I was really shook-up. Diggit, I knew I had lost weight every time I looked at my body or felt my muscles. But seeing myself in the mirror was something else. My face was like parchment, yellowish brown. My eyes were sunken in and had dark rings under them. There were remnants of a half-dozen pimples that had starved to death. My hair, never easy to control, had declared independence and each strand was striking out on its own.

I filled a cupped hand with water and began to wet my hair. After much dipping and plastering down, I looked something like a cadaver that still knew how to breathe. I checked my teeth, and their yellow color made me wonder if they had ever been white. I rinsed my mouth with water and polished and scraped with finger and nail. I spread my lips and made all kinds of faces inspecting my teeth. Not too bad.

I returned to the ward and for the first time saw guards checking things out. I had seen the cops before, but only under the influence of drugs, which had made the whole scene hazy.

"You finished yet?"

I nodded and walked up to Mrs. Hylton. "Here's the works," I said. She looked at the enema and pointed to the shelf where there were many others. "Put it there. If you want to, you can go over to recreation and pass the time."

I nodded thanks and began making my way up the corridor to the recreation room. There were offices and rooms on both sides, but only one exit, with the usual uniformed policeman guarding it from the outside. The door leading to the outside had glass panes, but it also had heavy steel bars to offset the brittleness. As I approached the recreation room, I noticed that just a little way beyond were some cages, not cells—cages, barred on all four sides. No matter where you stood, you could be seen from any side. The only contents were a bed and a bedpan, but one of the cages held a man. He was squatting in a corner, picking at his toes and mumbling inarticulately. *Observation cage*, my mind said.

I squinted for focus and saw the blurred outline of a policeman's uniform. I looked at the barred windows and a new feeling gripped my guts. *I'm really in here and no amount of make-believe can change that.* It was my imagination, of course, but the corridor seemed to get narrower and narrower, like I was headed toward a vanishing point. Patients and guards stared at me. They must have read the newspapers, too. As I got to the doorway leading to the recreation room, the blurred face of the policeman came more clearly into view.

"What the hell are you staring at me for, cop-shooter?" His voice sounded damn close. He wouldn't have cared even if I had told him I was damn near blind without my eyeglasses. He was just a blue blur against the light green wall paint. I walked on, nodding to a few patients when they nodded at me, and made my way over to a barred window where I looked down at the street below for the first time. I figured it was about eight stories down, a long way. I was skinny enough to fit through the bars, but I was sure as hell too damn weak to fly down to them streets. I stopped daydreaming and gazed about the recreation room. Fifteen or so patients were engaged in various activities, some playing checkers or chess, others playing cards, but most were watching TV.

"Hey, brother. Don't admit to nothing. You're innocent until proven guilty."

I recognized the voice of Fu Manchu.

"I got busted with smoking pistols."

He waved my excuse away. "Bullshit," he said, "circumstantial evidence. You could have picked the piece up after one of the stickup men dropped it."

Before I could answer, a loud, funny-sounding voice blared in my ear. "Damn right. Caught that woman of mine in bed with this other guy and..."

I took two steps backward and stared at a tall, oversized man with a wild look in his eyes. Fu Manchu, who was trying to reassure me everything was cool by making circles with his finger at the side of his head, leaned over confidentially and whispered, "Don't mind him. He's crazy."

"Why, I ripped them both open." His eyes opened wider and wider and insanity shone out of them. He put a heavy hand on my shoulder and my mouth jumped open.

"Hey, wait a minute, get your hands off me."

"I don't mean no harm," the wild-eyed man said soothingly in an effort to go on with his story. "I did a job on them like they was high-quality linoleum. Imagine, after eleven years of marriage she does this to me."

He was getting really uptight when two attendants came up, grabbed him, and led him away ranting, "Ya know what I did? Dammit to hell, I ripped them with my carpet-cutter..." His last words trailed off in the distance and I finished his sentence for him "...and laid them wall to wall." I shook my head from side to side in relief.

"Don't worry about nothing, brother," Fu Manchu reassured me and walked away.

"Thanks, bro. I won't." *Oh, shit!*

"Hebbin, Hebbin, Gonna Walk All over God's Hebbin"

There wasn't much to do except get medical checkups by the doctor, read, talk, listen and observe, and eventually it was all boring. The only things to take the edge off were the eternal whist and dirty hearts card games, checkers, and the half-busted TV. When it came right down to it, everything in that prison ward was boring, since all anybody could think about was getting the hell out of there.

I had finished lunch, which for me consisted of soup and mashed potatoes and gravy. My insides still hadn't graduated to digesting meat. I was trying to figure out what to do next, maybe another round of whist or checkers. I didn't want to lie down because that always started me thinking about the mess I was in. So I was headed for the recreation room when I heard my name called: "Peter Thomas." It was an attendant who motioned for me to come his way.

"What's up?" I asked.

"Visit—your aunt." He pointed to the little cubicle reserved for visits. I shuffled over to it, unable to see which aunt it was until I was peering at my Aunt Otilia through the wire-mesh partition. She smiled at me and I smiled back. Her eyes took me in and I could feel her intense gaze on all of me that was visible to her. Her face registered the shock of what she saw, a me that was wasted down to the bone, with my face so thin that my smile must have made it seem like a grinning skull. The smile on her lips dissolved to quivering pity, and sorrow nestled in the wrinkles of her face. Tears began to flow down her cheeks just like Momma's used to, a long, long time ago.

"Hey, Tía. Come on now." I grinned. "Everything's gonna be all right. *Por, Dios, Tía, no llores, lo siento que te he hecho sufrir—igualmente a los demás de la familia.* [Oh, God, Aunt, don't cry. I'm sorry I've made you suffer—the same for the rest of the family.]"

Tía's head bobbed up and down slowly, her face struggling to overcome her tears with a smile. Her lips parted and a warm smile shone through.

"Are you feeling *mejor?*"

"*Sí*, Tía. I'm much better. How are you?"

"Fine."

"And Trina?"

"*Bien. Todo bien.*" Too late, Tía sniffed back a tear.

"Don't you worry, Piri. The family is with you. We all love you very much. It is just that we can't understand why you did what you did."

I forced myself to smile and stared at her while trying to put together the reasons so we both would know. But I didn't say anything because she wouldn't understand. Anytime she had trouble, she'd turn to God and couldn't understand why I hadn't.

"*¿Por qué?*, Piri. *¿Por qué?*"

I shook my head from side to side and whispered, "*Porque el mundo es malo y uno tiene que ser malo para sobrevivir en él.* [Because the world is bad and one's got to be bad to survive in it.] That's why, Tía. You live in your house, you tend your job on the sewing machine, and then you split to church. Me, Tía, after the house, all I got is the streets. Aw, forget it, Tía. Square business. *No te apures.*"

"*Hijo*, we all got some money for a lawyer. Not much, but if we need more, we'll get it."

I wondered why I was choking up.

"I'll pay you all back sometime. Tell the family that."

"We don't want the money. We want you."

"I feel the same, Tía."

Her face started wrinkling up again. I forced a big smile and she forced one, too.

"Visit over," said a voice.

"I left you *cinco pesos* for what little things you need, *hijo*."

"*Gracias*, Tía. Tell everybody I'm all right."

"Everybody around the block sends you regards. Momma Julie, too. She is praying for you. She tried to come and see you but they won't let her in, only family. They didn't want to let me in, but I told them your mother is dead and you don't have family close by but me."

"Give them all my love, Tía. Tell Trina *que la amo*. [I love her.]"

Tía backed away, waving and pointing to the guard she'd left the money with as if to remind me I wasn't broke. I smiled and waved back, watching her grow smaller and disappear behind a heavy wooden door. I walked out of the visiting cubicle and leaned against the wall. Seeing Tía had made me happy; at last seeing someone of my blood, I didn't feel so damn alone.

So *why the hell do I feel so depressed?* My spirit was sinking clear down to my hospital slippers. "Aw, shit," I mumbled and shuffled off to the recreation room. A game of whist was going on between Fu Manchu and three other patients. After a couple of hands, Fu Manchu asked if I wanted to take his place for a while. I nodded, figuring it might get me out of the dumps. I mixed the cards and dealt.

"Saw you got a visit, bro," Fu Manchu prodded me.

I nodded yes and continued dealing.

"Your mother?"

"My aunt."

He shook his head sadly. "Yeah, it's tough when—"

"Damn, Fu Manchu." He was grinding me and my depression right into the ground. I wanted like all hell to curse the crap out of him, but instead I eased out from my chair and asked if he wanted to take over my hand.

"*Chevere*," Fu Manchu grinned and, studying my hand cheerfully, proceeded to bid four no trump down the river. I watched as he got completely wiped out.

His partner blew his cool. Fu Manchu laughed good-naturedly. "Aw, it's only a game. Only a fucking game. Nobody was putting anything up."

The cards were dealt, and Fu Manchu proceeded again to bid four no trump and without grinning went down the river and took every damn card. I walked away hearing him say something about when it's time for somebody to win, he'll win.

As I approached my bed, I recognized one of the plainclothesmen who had arrested me. He was talking with the doctor, but his eyes were running all over that open ward looking for someone. I nicknamed him "El Bull." His search stopped when he saw me and our eyes locked for a second. I shrugged and shuffled past him to my bed, bending over and hobbling more than necessary. I'd listened to lots of conversations that said the best strategy was to stay in the hospital as long as you could, 'cause if they get you in court while your name is still in the papers or even in the public's mind, you've had it as far as making a deal is concerned.

I made a big show of getting my ass back into bed, digging the plainclothesmen who were probably from the D.A.'s office. Staring up at the ceiling with my elbows shielding my eyes, I could watch them without their knowing it. They moved away from the doctor and headed for the exit, but not before one of them threw me a gesture with a kind of piranha grin that made it clear he'd be seeing me soon.

I wondered if it would be a good idea secretly to rip open my wounds. One prisoner had told me he'd done it to his stomach wound: "Like nothing to it, I just pulled my stitches apart, got the blood to running, and screamed like hell. It really looks worse than it is." Another prisoner threw in something about eating brown soap—you're sure to get the vomits and diarrhea. I had shaken my head nay at both pieces of advice, figuring that one gets that desperate only when facing a murder charge.

I waited for the doctor to come over and fill me in on what the plainclothesman wanted, but he wasn't breaking a leg getting over to me. So I got out of bed and nonchalantly made my way over to him.

"Good afternoon, Doc."

He merely nodded.

"Pretty busy, huh?"

He just ignored me. Like he was busy checking out a black youngster who had a knife slash across his belly that ran from the ward up to 110th Street. I peeked over the doctor's shoulder and dug about a million stitches that made the wound look like a giant centipede lying on its back. The dark catgut seemed to be wriggling like so many legs.

"Jesus Christ, what a mess," I said out loud, though I only meant to think it.

The doctor turned to me and said gently, "Will you get the hell out of here?"

"What did they want, Doctor?"

"Who, dammit, who?"

"Them guys you were talking to."

"Oh," he said, softly patting on the black youngster's white bandages. "They wanted to know how soon you'll be ready to leave. Seems you got an appointment with the court. They were asking if you were well enough to be checked into the Tombs."

"And?" I asked the doctor, hoping he'd noticed my greatly exaggerated weak condition. I didn't need to put on too much. I knew I looked and felt like something that didn't get scooped after the poop.

"Tomorrow, they'll be coming back. You're O.K. Just need to walk around more, eat a well-balanced diet, plenty of fresh air, rest, no worries, periodical checkups."

He moved away from me as Fu Manchu came up and asked, "What's happening?"

"I'm leaving tomorrow."

"Tough shit." He pulled a crumpled copy of the *Daily News* from under his arm and, clucking sadly, repeated, "Tough shit. Here, dig this."

I pulled the newspaper from him and put my nearsighted eyes a couple of inches away from the headlines, digging the front-page picture of some guys lying dead, shot up into Swiss cheese. I turned to the story on page two and quietly squinted to read how some guys had tried to pull a job in the Village.

"Just like you and your boys, right around the same area," broke in Fu Manchu. I kept reading.

"Just like you and your boys, except—" and Fu Manchu patted me in a brotherly fashion—" that you cats were lucky. I mean *luck-ee*."

I folded the newspaper without reading on.

"Man, tough shit," repeated Fu Manchu.

"Why?"

"Well, can't you see? I mean you ain't been here long enough for public opinion to die down, and these guys pulling the same kind of stickup in the same damn Greenwich Village section. Well, like it reminds them all over again."

"Aw, shut up," I snapped at him. "I need your information like a hole in the..."

"Sorry, *panín*. I wasn't putting words out to make you feel chopped out."

"Aw, it's O.K. Just the pressure's got me a little jumpy."

"Damn, Sam," Fu Manchu said, staring at the crumpled, bullet-riddled bodies on the front page. "Man, they sure hit them heavy. You really were lucky, *papo*. You must have a good spirit watching over you."

"I'm getting away from you, man. Like you're too heavy. You already got me thinking on how I can cop a connection with some foo-foo spirits." I turned and walked away.

I sat on my bed staring through the barred windows at the light-blue sky turning black. The city light bulbs were going on all over. Noises became acute in my ears. I heard car brakes screeching and horns screaming warnings. I heard patients lost in conversations, jailhouse lawyering, the business of how much heroin cost by the kilo on the underworld market. The lights in the ward went out and in the semidarkness I watched guards peek in from the outside and attendants and nurses doing their last-minute things. I shivered, not from the cold that always seemed to be a part of the

Bellevue Ward, but from the pounding pressure of the enormity of the bad-ass trouble I was in. It hadn't seemed real before. I was still weak, too filled with pills, but the stronger I got, the more lucid my mind became. My memories straightened out. The past caught up with me today and got ready to gang up on me tomorrow.

My thoughts were interrupted by someone singing, "Hebbin, Hebbin, gonna walk all over God's Hebbin." I looked at an old, thin black man; his pajama top was unbuttoned and his ribs stuck out so tightly against his wrinkled dark skin that it seemed they might push their way through at any moment. He was covered with beads of sweat, his eyes wide open and staring into nothing. He stopped singing and began to talk unintelligibly. I caught some of the words.

"Ah shunt be heah. Ah shunt be heah. Hebbin, Hebbin, gonna walk all over God's Hebbin."

I watched him reel like a drunk and wondered if he were crazy. He began to scream in a high-pitched voice that kept cracking with the effort. He began turning slowly round and round, lurching from side to side, and his sounds became a mixture of singing, mumbling, and screaming tears. His mouth opened wide in a grotesque yawn and he smiled at something only he could see. His few remaining teeth were yellowed with age. Nobody moved to help him. I just sat there with frozen eyes and shuddered involuntarily at the macabre human scene before me. Two men in white and a guard appeared and took hold of him. An attendant opened the door to one of the padded cells and the old man was taken inside, still screaming, still singing, still smiling. The cell door was flung shut and his agony was muffled to a lonely low tone.

Suddenly the ward sprang alive, as if the door closing on the old man released us all from the paralysis that had gripped us. Protests began to fill the ward.

"Hey, that man's sick, not crazy."

"Yeah, send for the doctor."

"Can't you see the man's got fever?"

My own voice joined in, "That old man can't hurt nobody. Can't you see something's wrong with him?"

The guards stood at alert. One of the attendants said, "We know what's wrong with him. You all don't. Best keep quiet. You all got enough trouble as it is."

The attendants and the guards walked away slowly. A few minutes later, lights again went out, leaving the ward engloomed in weak night lights. The muted agonies behind the padded door could still be heard: "Hebbin, Hebbin, gonna walk all over God's Hebbin."

That night I fell into a nightmare of bullets ripping me apart.

In the morning, when the padded cell was opened, the old man was lying in a corner, curled up in fetus position. He was dead. An attendant said it was from pneumonia. Goddamnit!

CHECKING OUT

"John Peter Thomas—John Peter Thomas."

I looked toward the voice, half-curious to find out how he knew my full name.

"Hey, your name John Peter Thomas?" He pointed a finger at me.

"Yeah," I replied.

"You're checking out today, buddy," the attendant said. "Let's go."

I waved to Fu Manchu, who squinted a smile and said, *"Buena suerte, panín."*

"Tu también." I followed the attendant. The gates opened as if by magic at the sight of the piece of paper in the attendant's hand. I noticed that he was almost my size and just about the same color. We went through one door after another. *If I can just get into his clothes, I could pass for him and walk right out of Bellevue flying free.* I kept eyeing him, trying to figure out how to get him to go peacefully into some closet and quietly change his clothes without hurting him. It never dawned on me that he could hurt me, even though I was down from 150 pounds of good hard weight to 70 pounds of skin and bones and he looked to be 170 pounds of jaw-cracking, ass-kicking, back-breaking health.

While I was still trying to make up my mind where to drag his unconscious body after I had chopped him down, he was already introducing me to a couple of detectives and somebody from the D.A.'s office. He went out and came right back with a large paper bag tagged with the name James Ford on a cardboard ID and cheerfully tossed it to me.

"Here you go, champ." His muscles rippled. I glared at

him with a look that said he didn't know how lucky he had been. He just stared at me as if he were viewing a hunk of skin and bones. Then, winking sympathetically, he wheeled around with the grace of a cat and split down his law-abiding path.

I quit fantasizing when El Bull's voice boomed at me. I remembered him wasting the side of my head and trying to break my fingers with his gun butt, screaming something about me not using that hand again. Only the ambulance doctor's intervention had saved me from a complete ripping-up, "Enough—that man is my patient."

"Get them goddamn clothes on fast," El Bull roared.

I noticed another detective with him. I pulled the string on the back of my hospital gown and stepped out of it. I scratched my balls in El Bull's direction without looking at him. He jumped red with anger.

"Goddammit, stop scratching your balls, you skinny-ass gorilla, and get your clothes on."

I stared at him, opened the paper bag, and pulled the clothes out. My blue doeskin suit was wrinkled and stiff with dried blood. I tried not to make a face as I crunched myself into my clothes, feeling the stiffness of the dried blood scratch against my skin. Then I heard something that made my insides freeze. Without looking at me, El Bull casually said to his buddy, "I don't know why they're gonna go through the bother of a trial. It's a waste of money. The cop he shot died yesterday morning. He's got the chair. I hope the hell it takes a long time for his goddamn ass to fry."

I buttoned my overcoat, searching in El Bull's face for a sign that he was kidding.

"I hear you feel it all the way—the first pains that come into your balls as they fry, and the shock is so bad you piss and shit on yourself." He still didn't look at me. "Too bad about Scotty. He was a good cop."

Maybe he's talking about somebody else.

"Yeah, you sonofabitch." He looked dead at me. "Too goddamn bad they can't fry your black ass twice, you miserable cop-killing bastard."

I heard my voice saying, "It shoulda been you that got it instead of him. At least he had heart, he fought it out, but you jumped yellow and dove for the bar. I saw you."

El Bull's face paled. He started for me. His buddy was quicker than he and held him back. El Bull just kept yelling, "I'll kill him, I'll kill him, so help me, I'll kill him."

"Control yourself, man," his buddy said.

El Bull pulled himself together, took a deep breath, and laughed. "Jesus Christ, I'm a damn fool for letting that bastard get to me."

Our eyes met and his told me that I shouldn't ever get taken alive by him, no time, nowhere.

We went down in the elevator to street level and walked slowly through the corridor. El Bull's eyes never left me. As we got near the exit, he put out an arm and blocked my way, then pulled out a piece of chain, twisted it around my skinny wrist, and held the ends tightly in a closed fist. Attached to each end was a vertical metal bar for better grip. I was used to regular handcuffs. This was new.

Out in the street the cold air ripped right through my clothes. My teeth began to clatter like marbles. The plainclothesmen walked me over to a police van. Suddenly I saw a man running across the street.

"Hey, wait a sec. Hey, hold on." The running figure came up close, puffing out cold white clouds of steam. He had a camera.

"Hey, fellers. Just a couple of pictures, O.K.? I'm with a crime magazine. Just a couple. Be a good kid, O.K.?" He lifted his camera and I gave him my back.

"Hey, come on, just a couple of pictures. Is it all right, fellers?"

He asked El Bull, who broke into a Hollywood smile and nodded, "Yeah, why not?"

Somebody put a hand on me to pull me back. I jerked away. Then I heard it. "You goddamn dirty nigger, you goddamn sonofabitch. Let me see your fucking black face."

The racial insults slammed into my back. I turned and felt my face twist into a snarl. My mouth opened and hurled a torrent of curses.

"Gotcha," the photographer smiled sweetly and added good-naturedly, "Thanks a lot, kid. No hard feelings. Got a job to do."

He split across the street, whistling. Through the steel mesh of the back door of the police van, I saw streets, and people dodging cars, and clumps of dirty snow turning into slush.

"Jesus, I forgot to ask him what magazine he works for and when it's coming out," said El Bull.

"What are you, a celebrity now?" his partner said, laughing. "You sure are going Hollywood."

"I noticed you weren't hiding your shit-eating grin behind your hat," replied El Bull.

They both laughed. I lost myself in thoughts, wondering what was ahead of me.

ARRAIGNMENT

The paddy wagon stopped and El Bull twisted the chain around my wrist. I got out and looked at the building before me. It was a police station.

"Hey," I said to anyone. "I thought we were supposed to go to the Tombs."

"We're going there soon enough, killer. But first we'd like to ask you some questions."

El Bull tugged at my wrist chain. "Let's go."

We went into a police station that must have been built around 1890. The bright sunlight outside didn't want no part of the inside of that station 'cause it was as dark and hard-looking as one of them bad-ass after-hours joints in Harlem.

I was led up a long flight of steps by El Bull and his partner. I gripped my butterfly stitch 'cause all the climbing was sure as hell gonna jar the shit outta me. Halfway up or so, I stopped to rest. El Bull just watched me and his big blue eyes told me I wasn't getting a shit-hill-of-beans help from him.

"Ya gotta strong heart, spic. I figured them steps might of sent you bye-bye."

I started to say something smart but bit my tongue. Instead, I innocently scratched between my legs.

"Whatcha got, crabs or something?" El Bull roared.

"Search me," I answered gently.

El Bull threw up his arms.

"I'll kill him, so help me God. I'll kill him, Fred."

"Take it easy, buddy. Take it easy. Go out for some coffee or something. I'll take care of him."

El Bull went out, still cursing. I was left alone with Fred, who sat on the edge of his desk, folded his arms, and silently observed me, not mean or mad, but maybe trying to figure what was inside me.

"How old are you?"

"Twenty-two." I just stared at him.

"I want to ask you some questions. Cooperate and everything will be fine. I don't want my buddy to question you."

I nodded yes.

"Did you pull a job on August 6, a delicatessen on West Eighty-fourth Street?"

I shook my head no.

"How about three Gristede Brothers markets in September?"

No again from me. His voice became dim as I turned him off. He mentioned hotel stickups, liquor stores, muggings. I kept shaking my head no.

"You didn't do any of these?" His voice was still gentle.

"This is my first job." I looked him straight in the eyes.

El Bull came roaring in and began slamming chairs and pounding on the desk with his fist.

"You got two fuckin' seconds to start coming up with some answers."

"Jesus, I feel pretty lousy," I said to no one in particular. "I think I'm gonna throw up."

I didn't look at either of the detectives. They would have read the bullshit in my eyes.

"Oh, for Christ's sake. Uncuff the son of a bitch before he shits up the office."

I was taken to the toilet. As I started to close the door of the stall, El Bull pushed it open.

"For crying out loud, buddy," Fred said, "where the hell can he go? Down the shit bowl?"

"I ain't taking my fucking eyes off him. Go ahead, throw up, you skinny-ass gorilla."

I bent over the toilet bowl and made all kinds of noises in my throat. *Jesus, man, I really don't feel like throwing up. He's gonna know I was bullshitting and wipe up the toilet with me.* I worked up all the saliva I could and let it out, hoping it'd look like some kind of vomit.

"Is that all? Some kind of spit?"

I wiped my mouth with the back of my hand and looked at him, hoping my face had the sick look of somebody who had just vomited.

"It's all I got in me, man. I ain't been eating much." I tried a weak burp. El Bull glared at me and turned away.

"Bring him back into the office, Fred, before I stuff his black ass down that shit bowl and flush him to hell."

I adjusted my clothes and walked on ahead of Fred. I got handcuffed to my chair.

"We're gonna ask you questions again and this time there better be some answers." The voice sounded much meaner, like Fred really wasn't friendly anymore.

El Bull sat looking at me from across his desk, his right elbow propped on it, while he massaged his tight lips back and forth with his fist.

"Are you ready to answer?" Fred asked.

I nodded a big yes. For the next fifteen minutes, every unsolved stickup that had been pulled, I admitted pulling.

"Gristede Brothers?" asked Fred.

"Yes."

"A & P Market?"

"Yes."

"Lerner's Liquor Store?"

"Yeah, that too."

"Whalen's Drug Store?"

"Uh-huh."

El Bull turned livid with rage and Fred had to hold him back for real.

"You goddamn skinny-ass gorilla. Who the hell you think you're playing with? Every stickup we asked you about, you admitted doing. Some of them happened at the same goddamn time in different parts of the city. "Oh, you little sonofabitch, you got an ass-whipping coming."

I looked at El Bull and said, "Well, if I said no to having pulled them stickups, you were gonna whip my ass, wasn't you? So—I said yeah to all of them."

El Bull grabbed me by the front of my shirt.

"Take it easy, buddy," Fred got in between. "He's got a whole lot of time coming just on this bust alone, enough to pay for the other ones he thinks he's getting away with."

"Bullshit. This shit ain't getting time. He's getting the chair."

"For what?" It slipped out of Fred.

I caught the look on El Bull's face. Fred had blown the jewels. *Nobody's dead. I'm not gonna fry.* It was just El Bull's way of getting his kicks, like tearing butterfly wings off for fun.

"Let's get him down for arraignment."

I was taken from the police station to 100 Centre Street and put into a large cell known as "the bull pen," where about ten other prisoners were awaiting their time in court. I sat down on a long bench, leaned against the wall, and watched prisoners go to court. Some came back to the bull pen, some didn't. I overheard a voice saying, "Well, lucky Max got bailed out." After about half an hour my name was called.

"Peter Thomas." The guard's voice sounded impatient.

"Yeah?"

"Let's go—get the lead out." The guard ushered me out of the world of gray bars into one of long wooden benches and wood-paneled walls, the courtroom. There the guard nudged me impatiently to let me know I was to look at the judge and nothing else. My ears picked up my violent accomplishments being read off:

"John Peter Thomas, alias Pedro González, alias James Ford; you are hereby charged with attempted armed robbery in the first degree, felonious assault with intent to kill, and illegal possession of firearms. How do you plead?"

I swear it was hard to believe it was me that was being charged with all that shit. I stared at the judge. He stared at me and repeated, "How do you plead, guilty or not guilty?"

"Do you understand English?" someone asked.

Hell, yes, I thought. *I was born in Harlem Hospital. How much more American can you get?*

"Yes, I can," I answered instead.

The judge looked around. "Is there a Legal-Aid lawyer present?"

Someone came forward.

"This court will appoint a lawyer to represent you until such time as you are able to have one of your own preference. Understand?"

A young white guy smiled at me and whispered into my ear. "I'm Mr. Lubell. Just say 'Not guilty.'"

"Not guilty," I said clearly.

"The day for the defendant's court appearance for trial will be two weeks from today."

Mr. Lubell spoke up. "Your Honor, I would appreciate it if the court would set a reasonable bail for my client."

A man in a neat gray suit who had been seated at a table in front of the judge now rose and said, "Your Honor, the state urges the court, because of the gravity of the charges, to set the bail for the defendant at one hundred thousand dollars!"

Damn, that can't be right, I thought. He must have said one hundred dollars.

The judge rapped his gavel. "Bail for the defendant is set at one hundred thousand dollars. Bailiff, please remove the prisoner."

Oh, shit. The judge gotta be crazy. Je-suss. If I had a hundred gees, would I the fuck be here?

"Let's go," said the bailiff, nudging my elbow.

I was taken back to the bull pen and held there until the last prisoner had seen the judge. Then a guard yelled out, "Everybody out, come on. Let's move it." And ten minutes later we were entering a mile-high building at 125 White Street. It was the Tombs.

A Tomb for the Living

El Bull nudged me toward the entrance. Inside was a metal gate. The guard waited until El Bull presented his identification, then opened up and handed him some papers to sign. I looked around as El Bull removed my handcuffs and couldn't help but notice how dark and gloomy the place was. Without saying a word to me, El Bull turned and walked out. I almost missed his presence; he was a familiar sight to me and this place was strange turf.

"Empty your pockets," said the guard.

I emptied my pockets of some small change, nine one-dollar bills, half a pack of tailor-mades (regular smokes), matches, and some Juicy Fruit gum. Another guard came up and stood by while the first gave me a thorough search.

"O.K., you're clean," he said, stepping back. I reached for my property and he checked me by saying, "Take only your cigarettes and gum. I will check your money in your account. You can draw two bucks a day for commissary. Sign here for your money."

I reached for the cigarettes and gum but was beaten to them by the second guard, who, as an afterthought, decided to search them. I figured it had to be for drugs or money 'cause sure as hell I couldn't hide a hacksaw blade or gun in them. As I was led to the elevator, the second guard said, "Hold it," and handed me two heavy gray blankets. The elevator stopped on the eighth floor of the Tombs and I was taken up a metal staircase to what was called the second tier and locked in a cell with a bunk bed, no mattress, a wash bowl, and a toilet bowl without a top. The cell was about six feet wide, eight long, and about nine high. I started to put one of the heavy blankets on the bed as a mattress when the cell started to spin round and round. I felt nauseous and little lights began to blink on and off in front of my eyes like Fourth of July sparklers. I stumbled around groaning from the burning pain in my guts.

Dimly I heard a voice yelling, "Hang up, hang up," and wondered who was taking the shortcut home. Footsteps approached, and looking up, I saw a guard observing me. He was staring at my chest. A little dribble of blood was seeping from underneath my butterfly stitches. He went away and twenty minutes later came back to take me from my cell. "I got the O.K. to put you on murderers' row down on the flats," he said. "You won't have to climb stairs and we can keep a better eye on you, just in case..." He left the rest hanging.

My head felt light, and in between the dull thumpings of pain in my chest I wondered if the real reason for my being put on murderers' row was that the detective I had shot was dead after all and it was gonna be game time from now on. It was some comfort to recall that the detective Fred had given the lie to El Bull's assertion about their colleague's dying.

I was brought to a cell on the flats. My shoestrings and belt were taken from me, a rule on murderers' row to prevent prisoners from committing suicide and thereby cheating the state of its due.

My nerves were begging for nicotine. I closed my eyes for a long while to shut out the lack of space and the abundance of time. When I opened them again, the lights had gone out in my cell.

"Damn, what a fucking time for a light bulb to blow out," I grumbled out loud.

"It's lights-out time, buddy," said a voice from the next cell.

"What time is it?" I closed my eyes again.

"Who the hell cares?" he said. "What are you in for?"

"Stickup," I replied.

I wished I had a cigarette. I'd smoked my last in the cell upstairs.

"Say, you got a match?" I asked.

"Yeah, bro." His hand bearing the matches appeared in my cell.

"You got a smoke to go with it?" I hoped he had a sense of humor. He did.

"Hey, that's a new way to hustle a tailor-made. Here you go. Here's a couple to hold you till tomorrow."

"Thanks a lot, bro. Good looking out."

"No sweat. Shit, a cat could go crazy locked up in this birdcage without no pot. If it wasn't for cigarettes…"

I lit my cigarette, inhaled deeply, and damn near busted open my insides from a coughing fit that took a couple of minutes to subside. *Coño, I gotta watch that shit.* I pressed the button in the wash bowl and downed water from my open palm, then moved over to the bars, leaned against them, and stared at tremendous windows thirty or forty feet high. Behind them was the city, but the panes were opaque. I took a drag on the cigarette and rolled the smoke around my mouth before letting it out. The only sound in the echoing vastness of the Tombs seemed to be the heels and soles of the innocent-until-proven-guilties pacing up and down. The cigarette got flicked into the toilet bowl and I lay down to escape into sleep.

Next morning, I woke up to the crashing sound of cell doors opening and closing and the smell of coffee and old sweat. As I eased out of bed, a man dressed in gray was pushing trays of breakfast underneath the gate of each cell. A tray slid along the concrete floor into my cell.

"Breakfast," intoned a cheerful voice. I stared down at the tray. *Are we animals locked in a pen?* I wondered how I could get it without having to bend down like a dog. I got a mental picture of prisoners in their cells, down on all fours, slurping away like skinny ghetto hounds. I was determined not to bend my knees to pick up that tray. I stretched out on the bed and pulled the tray to me, then making a one-hand press, lifted it onto my cot and wolfed down the food.

After a while, the inmate messman came around asking if anybody wanted firsts on coffee. I nodded and he said, "Gimme your cup." I held the cup to the bars and he poured scalding hot coffee from the spout of a large metal container.

"You want seconds on oatmeal?"

"Nay," I said and went on drinking the volatile brew.

Someone screamed out orders and a voice in the next cell said, "That hack's a sonofabitch."

"Hack's bad, huh?" I asked.

"As bad as that blackjack he calls Rosie lets him be."

The lock was sprung and my cell door slid open. I stepped out into the narrow walk space. To the right and left of me for as far as I could see on one side of the wall were cells. On the other side, a metal ledge ran along the length of the cellblock; behind it were the large opaque windows.

I stood in the narrow space and watched the cells yield up other human beings, all shapes, ages, and colors, but mostly black and Puerto Rican.

Card games were quickly formed on the ledge and I picked up conversations about all kinds of problems, but nary a declaration of guilt. Some of the guests merely came out, looked around, and went back in their cells to plop on their bunks. I eased myself gingerly back on my bed and sat there with hands folded between my legs. I watched the life swarming around me like ants on an anthill. I looked at the tall barred windows and strained hard as hell to see through them. *No use. Nobody inside is gonna see out and nobody is ever gonna see in.*

"Hey, kid, wanna use the mop?"

I checked out the voice—an old white guy who looked like he'd been in and out of jailhouses since the beginning of time.

"What for?" I asked, coming out on the walk space.

"To clean your cell."

"Thanks. I don't need the mop. My room is clean."

"It's rules, buddy. Cells got to be cleaned whether they need it or not."

I stared at the old man. "Look. I don't need to mop. Now check out."

"Yes, you do need the mop," a voice came from the side. It was the hack who hung around with a blackjack named Rosie. Our eyes locked together and little warning bells went off in my head. *Better reconsider the need of a mop.*

El Hack just stood there, stern, immovable, staunch and sturdy as a johnny pump on 109th Street. I looked at the old man, who was now offering me the mop with all kinds of secret signals. By this time, other bustees and some guards were looking my way.

"Your cell is filthy," El Hack hissed.

"I thought I cleaned it," I said, remembering the itty-bitty piece of dust I had wiped away. "But"—and I looked around, *mucho* cool, but sweating my ass off on account of that Rosie blackjack in El Hack's right hand—"I'm for things being clean."

"One more word out of you..."

I took the mop from the old man and walked into my cell as straight as my butterfly stitch would allow me. I mopped, and felt eyes staring.

"What's that cat in for?"

"Man, he's supposed to be involved with some other cats in a stickup that ended up in a motherfucking shoot-out."

"Shit, he don't look that bad."

"Sucker, how bad do you have to look to pull a fucking trigger?"

I smiled and mopped away. *You don't have to look bad at all man, not bad at all.*

DEAD TIME IN
A DEAD END

Some prisoners in the Tombs actually breathed a sigh of relief after being sentenced to their terms. The pressure of waiting in agonizing uncertainty in the cramped quarters of the Tombs made it almost all right to go to prison, anything, as long as they got the hell out of there.

There were men in the Tombs who had been awaiting disposition of their cases for two and three years. That's worse than being in prison upstate 'cause it's pulling time without ever seeing the sky.

As the days wore on, the routine that was new for me at the beginning became increasingly, painfully boring. Guilty or innocent, the boredom was so great that before you knew it, if you weren't mentally strong enough, you'd be willing to cop out to 'most any plea and almost gladly accept years in prison just to get out and see any kind of green grass or white snow or gray slush.

The days dragged by for me slow as a sick turtle, and the routine was always the same—signing a voucher on your account the day before, getting two dollars in silver the next morning, then making it to the commissary wagon when it stopped outside the barred gate of the cellblock. You could pick up smokes, newspapers, toothbrush, toothpaste, coffee, cake, and candy—if you had money, of course. Otherwise, if you had no pride, you could hustle and cop extras even if they came entwined with a whole lot of insults. That wasn't my stick, but I'd watch cats who didn't have pride and when they hustled, it would be given to them with the same attitude people give a bum a handout on the Bowery.

There was shave and haircut time, when an outside barber came in and did service for cheap. The only thing your money could buy was a half-ass fifty-cent haircut and twenty-five-cent shave with a razor blade that had scraped beard and skin from the twenty guys before you. I caught a face infection and asked for some rubbing alcohol, but got a dirty look instead, like didn't I know it was drinkable and the state wasn't passing out any free drinks? I was given some antiseptic by the Tomb's doctor.

The monotony was broken up by the tortured entertainment of junkies kicking cold turkey, screaming in their misery and groaning helplessly when a guard sloshed buckets of cold water on them as a quick cure for their *mucho* bag-a-day habit...or cats going off their rockers and being put into straitjackets so they wouldn't present any danger as blackjacks bounced off their flesh and bones.

I passed time picking up prison terminology so I wouldn't be taken for a first-timer in the place. I figured it would also be useful in whatever prison house I'd be going to.

There was a prisoner named Tank, a former prize-fighter who was a wealth of terms like "hack" and "screw" (guards), "undercover faggot," and "short heist" (masturbation). I quit talking to him when he brought out the fact that he had read about me in the papers. I guess he meant no harm when he said, "Hey, man, I don't envy you one fuckin' bit. When you hit prison upstate, them guards are gonna know from your record you tried to waste a cop. They can get heavy-handed. Je-suss, like they don't go for cop-shooters."

I just stared at him for a hard while and walked away.

One day the guard handcuffed me to another prisoner and left the cuff fairly loose. I had lost so much weight, it was no sweat to slip it off my wrist. I did just that, simply to see if I could do it, then caught the cop watching me. I slipped it back on my wrist, clamped it tight, and kept walking.

One would think prisoners would get tired of talking over their cases with each other. On the contrary. It seemed discussing cases was the only means of knowing you had some importance, if only to the State of New York. Any prisoner with even a faint reputation as a jailhouse lawyer was kept busy trying to answer legal questions, like "What's the maximum time one can get by copping out to assault in the second degree?" or, "What was the best way to beat a rap based on circumstantial evidence?" or, "What's the most that can be gotten for bigamy?"

The homosexuals always complained that their bust was jive-ass and the law had no business sticking its nose into their private sex lives. The only prisoners who never discussed their cases were rapists, child molesters, and cats who were really up to their necks in and out of murder. Then there were the hard-faced, tight-lipped, well-dressed prisoners whose expensive cologne tagged them as boys *de la* Mafia. It was one hell of a mixture of humanity; name the crime and you'd find somebody facing time for it.

One day I was at the end of the cell hall washing my undershirts and shorts with brown soap in a bucketful of hot water. I was trying to make rhythm as I rubbed the articles of clothing together, anything to make it entertaining, when I heard a commotion.

"Get your motherfucking hands off me!" I recognized the voice of a dark-skinned Puerto Rican of about twenty-five years, named Chico.

"Get back in your cell," said a second voice, which belonged to the guard who was handy with the blackjack.

"Just get your hands off me. You got no goddamn right to be putting your fucking hands on me. I wasn't doing nothing but playing goddamn cards and this motherfucker tried to cheat."

Chico spit in the direction of a black cat of about thirty who was looking hurt and outraged at being called a card cheat.

"That's your business. Now stop cursing and get in your cell." The guard shoved Chico hard.

"I told you not to lay your fucking hands on me," Chico said, literally jumping a foot off the floor in rage. At that moment the guard clobbered him across a shoulder with his blackjack. *Whap!* Then the weapon caught Chico across the face as he spun in slow motion. The second whap and three or four pushes slammed Chico back into his cell. I moved to where I could see him.

Chico was neither conscious nor unconscious. He was slumped down on his bunk, wiping the flowing blood from his head and nose and rubbing its thickness between his fingers. We all went back to whatever we had been doing, mumbling and grumbling, but nothing else. There was no unity in the Tombs in 1950.

Rumors always fly around in a place where you can't get firsthand news of what's happening. Some cats were said to have hanged themselves and others were allegedly hanged by the guards. I never saw a guard hang a prisoner, but I sure as hell saw hacks playing bongo beats on a lot of guys' heads. In 1950, all the guards were white except for one or two blacks. There were no Puerto Rican guards. It was a very lop-sided employee ratio since the great majority of those awaiting trial were black or Puerto Rican. And like if there were certain white ethnic groups who didn't dig us on the outside, imagine how easy it was for them to get their jollies off in the controlled atmosphere of the Tombs.

Most of us had not been to trial yet, but, guilty or innocent, that didn't seem to cut any ice with the guards. To the last man, we were all guilty. Not talking about me, because I got busted with smoking pistols, but I think that somewhere among all us men and boys in the Tombs there had to be some who were innocent. And any quick checkout would show that the majority of the inmates were black or Puerto Rican from the different ghettos of New York. We had tried to get out of the ghetto by what we thought were the only available means.

I was sitting on the long bench playing cards when I heard my name called.

"Your lawyer wants to see you."

Five minutes later I sat across the table from my lawyer, separated by a low wooden partition. He smiled friendly-like and asked, "How you doing?"

"Beautiful. Can't you see?" I smiled politely. "What's new?"

"Well," he stretched that word out, "you pulled some other stickups in the Bronx, didn't you?"

"What the hell are you talking about?" I looked innocently at him.

"One of your partners turned state's evidence in return for a better deal for himself."

He went on to describe the two stickups and I knew he knew.

"If it makes you feel better, it was the one called Louis."

"Oh, shit." I got a mental picture of Louie, a tall, slim, white Puerto Rican, about twenty-three, who was my tight *amigo* buddy.

"So where does that leave me?" I asked.

"The Bronx district attorney's office is trying to make a deal with the Manhattan district attorney's office for them to give you a suspended sentence on the serious charges against you and then turn you over to the Bronx court. It seems they figure the most you get here in Manhattan, on account of your being a first offender, is fifteen years maximum on the attempted armed robbery and assault. But if you get a suspended sentence here, the Bronx office could try you as a second offender on first-degree armed robbery and put you away for a neat thirty to sixty years."

I held my breath as I calculated how much time that would mean. I'd be eighty-two years old when I got out if I pulled every day of it. I remembered a joke about Willie Sutton that I heard from a cat in the cell next to mine. *A guy gets converted, see, and sentenced to 150 years by the judge. He turns all kinds of colors and sputters, "For God's sake, Judge. I can't pull all that time." And the judge says, "That's all right. Do what you can while you're still alive. You can owe the state the rest."*

"Are you listening?" Mr. Lubell's voice broke up my running-around thoughts.

"Yeah, yeah, Mr. Lubell."

"I stopped them on the grounds that Manhattan has the original jurisdiction over you since you were arrested in this borough during the commission of a crime, and therefore the Bronx has to wait until you've paid your debt here first. You might as well know that the limit is fifteen years. I'm working on a five-year minimum and a fifteen-year maximum. The prosecutor is pushing for seven and a half to fifteen or better. You're going to be sentenced on two different charges. The felonious assault is good for an extra ten-year maximum. I'm working to get the two sentences to be served concurrently. You'll be serving both sentences together. If the prosecutor had his way, you'd serve one sentence first and then start on the next. So if you know how to pray or whatever, now's a good time to check out just how good your standing is with whoever watches over kids like you."

I shook my head and said, "Well, do the best you can, Mr. Lubell."

We stood up and he put out his hand. I shook it, and as an afterthought, asked, "You couldn't get them to set the bail down from a hundred thousand to a few hundred, could you?"

He shook his head and softly said, "Kid, when they gave you a hundred-thousand dollar bail it was to make sure that you would stay put."

I nodded.

"You'll be up for sentencing soon. What else can I tell you? See you then, huh?"

A few days later, I was visited by a probation officer who asked me questions dating back to age three.

"You might as well tell me the truth..." he said.

I studied him. He was about thirty years old, white and overweight, with a prematurely receding hairline. His nervous movements made me wonder if it was me or the Tombs that had him so uptight.

"...because I'll find it all out when I make my investigation into your home life and around your community."

I told him what he wanted to know, like information about my family and schooling. He even asked if I had anyone who would give character references "one way or the other." I gave him my family and Trina—like she'd do good by me and not screw up my character. When he had finished grilling me, he got up and said, "You'd better have told me the truth."

"Yes, sir," I smiled.

"You'd better had, 'cause when my report is finished it goes up before the sentencing judge, and it could be instrumental one way or the other."

I almost crossed my heart and did a hope-to-die-if-I'm-lying. I shook my head up and down in yes-time. I didn't dig his repeating his "one way or the other."

Another thing that broke up the routine was my psychological evaluation. A woman psychologist got me to playing with square and round blocks and wanted to know what various ink splotches looked like to me. She grunted when I told her they looked like what they were, "ink splotches." She seemed unhappy, so I tried to please her by saying some looked like wolves, others like butterflies, and for diversion, I said one looked particularly like a vagina. She glanced up from her ink splotches and seemed interested. I went back to animals, birds, and bees. I was in enough trouble without being put down on the record as obsessed with vaginas.

My day of sentencing was short and sweet. Five to fifteen years at hard labor for first degree armed robbery, and five to ten years at hard labor for first degree felonious assault with intent to kill. Then came words that were like a birthday present: "to be served concurrently." *Jesus, that means together. I'll be serving two days in one.* "You will be taken to Sing Sing Prison at Ossining..." and the rest was lost in a blur.

SING SING AIN'T
NO SONG

It was July, 1950, and from the moment the prison van drove away from Sing Sing State Prison at Ossining, New York, and the huge steel gate slammed behind me with finality, I felt helpless. The walls around the prison were gigantic with their buttresses and towers placed strategically all around the top. The guards in their dark-blue ties and uniforms seemed to be part of the fortress. Their heads revolved in a continuous 360-degree circumference. I heard a prisoner mumble something about this being the hour of "Do Right."

We were taken into a large room where there were four guards.

"All right, let's straighten out," yelled a guard.

We all almost snapped to some kind of attention.

"Hey, straighten up, you." The strong, clipped voice belonged to a top brass because there were captain's bars on his shoulders. It was me he was looking at. I winced inside and straightened out despite the pain from my wounds. A young black kid next to me whispered something to a white kid next to him. The white kid responded and the roaring explosion of El Captain's vocal chords shook the shit out of the room we were standing in.

"WHO THE HELL GAVE YOU PERMISSION TO SPEAK? WHO? GODDAMNIT!"

He took a hard look at us and began to speak, staccato-like.

"You men might as well get this straight. You're here

because you goddamn well deserve to be. You're here because society has found you not fit to live among it. If you want, it can be the toughest goddamn bit you inmates will ever pull. You'll be given rule books. Memorize them and follow them to the letter and you won't have any trouble getting along in here. Break them and the roof will come down on your heads so fast it will make you spin. The first rule is you give total respect to every official of this institution. There are all kinds of opportunities here to learn trades. Take advantage of them. You can either do the time or the time will do you. All right, Sergeant, they're all yours."

"Left, turn," said the sergeant in a matter-of-fact voice.

There was a moment of confusion. El Captain had shaken up some of us so bad that it took us a few seconds to find our left side.

"O.K., let's go," said the sergeant. "March, hup, two, three, four."

A gate opened and we marched down a long hall. A guard opened another gate and we were marched into a large room that had an inmate behind a counter.

"O.K., men. Strip off all your clothes and take them over to that man there." He pointed at the gray-garbed inmate. "He'll put your civilian clothes in a box and you can have them sent to your families, or we will dispose of them for you."

I almost didn't mind getting out of my clothes. The bullet holes in them and the bloodstains that remained despite my washing the hell out of them at the Tombs made me feel queasy all the time I wore them. I took them off and stood in line with the rest of the convicts. It's a funny feeling, being buck-ass naked in front of strangers in prison.

"Here you are, young fellow." The gray-garbed inmate had hair that matched his clothes. I wondered how many years he had been in and if my sentence of fifteen years at hard labor would age me faster and make me look like him before I got out?

"Just put them in this box and write out who you want it sent to." He smiled, and if he had six teeth left in his whole mouth, it was a lot.

"How long you in for, sonny?"

"Fifteen years max." I stared at him.

The old man let out a little giggle and said, "Listen, sonny, if I was you, I'd send them home. If you pull your whole fifteen years, these clothes are gonna be out of style anyhow."

I grunted an O.K. and wrote down my Tía Angelina's address, mulling over and over the old man's attempt at humor. *Jesus, the cat's right.*

I tucked my shoes under my arms and heard the sergeant's matter-of-fact voice.

"Check them too, feller. The state's gonna give you everything you'll need from now on."

I checked them.

"Line up."

We lined up.

"Right, turn. Straight ahead to the showers." And we walked to a long row of open shower stalls. Three inmate attendants waited there with towels neatly stacked in front of them. They looked at us with knowing smiles. I ignored them but kept them under observation. It didn't take long for them to start making remarks.

"Wowee, will you look at that little white kid's ass-cunt. That's a cherry if I ever saw one."

"Hey," said another sick voice, "cop a look at the fat ass on that one. Hairy as a jungle pussy."

"Naw, I'm for that white ass. Damn, I bet his ass would be tight as a sixteen-year-old virgin."

And funny squeaky noises began to come from their pursed lips, the sound of inhaled air forced between their teeth.

"Cut that crap," said the sergeant in his never changing matter-of-fact voice, but without really caring if it went on or not. "You men, into the showers."

As I stepped into the shower, a voice said, "Hey, skinny. You mind? Say, whatcha got that bandage on your chest for? Some nasty man bite you?"

I began soaping up, but I leaned out of the shower stall and made an up-your-ass gesture by wiggling my bent elbow up in the air. I checked the sergeant out. He was far over to one side, smoking a pipe. I thought of an answer I'd heard in the Tombs.

"Listen, motherfucker. I'm a man, diggit? I came in here my father's son and I'll be damned if I go out my mother's daughter."

"Everybody out. Everybody out," the sergeant roared.

We all lined up, rubbing ourselves dry. One of the asshole artists walked along in front of us, collecting the wet towels. As he reached for the towels, it was like the bare-asses were of one mind—we dropped our towels on the floor, forcing the sickie to bend over for each one, and made whispered remarks only for his ears about his questionable manhood.

As the asshole artist picked up the last towel, even the nervous white kid joined in.

"Ya mudderfucker. You so fucking ugly. I don't see how anybody could shit on you, let alone look at you."

Everyone cracked up at the kid's bravado, and the asshole artist split over to his clique, muttering threats.

"O.K., everybody this way."

We followed El Sergeant into another room where there were some officers along with El Captain.

"O.K., everybody bend over and grab your ankles."

"What the fuck is this?" a bare-ass whispered, ever so low.

"Don't tell me the hacks are fruity, too?"

"Naw, it's just an asshole inspection to check if you're carrying."

"Shut up there," said El Sergeant. "This here is to find out if you're carrying contraband in your rectums."

"Holy Mother of Christ," came a groaned whisper. "Ain't nothing sacred?"

"SPREAD YOUR BUTTS!"

All the butts spread. The inspection team stopped at each "tooshie," gave a grunt, and granted permission to stand straight again.

"O.K. Left, turn. Follow me."

We followed El Sergeant, who led us to a room where all sorts of prison-gray clothing were stacked.

"Give the clerks your sizes."

We copped our clothes. My prison shirt was brown and had the number 109669 stenciled on it. We were told we'd be given gray shirts when we became part of the prison population. We dressed and twenty minutes later were marched to segregation quarters and placed in our cells. We were given food and each of us ate lost in thought. Afterward, I lay back on the funky mattress. The white kid was bragging about how he had told the asshole artist off about "let alone somebody shitting on his face," and a more experienced voice came back, "yeah, kid, we heard you, but like you ain't heard his answer, yet."

I conked out. *What a hard-ass day!*

The next two weeks were taken up by a series on prison indoctrination with a combination prison guard-civilian teacher who put down the facts of what prison life was all about—the goodies that were in store for us via rehabilitation if we behaved ourselves and the head-cracking if we didn't behave as good cons should. He didn't sound mean, he just sounded like he'd said it hundreds of times. He went on to say there were all sorts of courses, vocational and academic, and an opportunity for dropouts to earn a high-school diploma. He asked how many of us had a high-school diploma, and out of about thirty, only two or three Einsteins raised their hands. I made up my mind to cop me a high-school diploma.

During those two weeks, we also filled out dozens of forms—what we'd like to study, what we'd like to work as—took an I.Q. test and some psychological evaluations, and had an interview with a psychiatrist who wanted to know if I dug my father more than my mother. There were medical check-ups, complete with chest X-rays, and I asked for eyeglasses, which I had done without since my own had been broken in the stickup. I was given an eye test and told I'd have to wait for new glasses.

Some of the two weeks' time in segregation was spent by most of us getting to know each other as well as one can get to know another con in the can. Some cons were close-mouthed, not unfriendly, just natural loners. I could understand them, since I was something like that. I got to know guys like Bayamon, Pancho, Zorro, Gordo, who were Puerto Ricans like me, and L'il Henry and Karl, who were black, and Johnny Lee and Checkers, who were white. A clique isn't made up; it just naturally forms itself by mutual acceptance. The worst part of the two weeks of orientation was the long stretches of cell time, eighteen or so hours a day. We couldn't wait to get out among the general population, no matter what it held. It was alive out there and not as buried as we were.

Finally, the two weeks were up.

"Hey, Piri, we'll be out in the population tomorrow. What job you get?"

I recognized the voice as Bayamon's. In the two weeks of orientation, we had gotten to know each other fairly well.

"I got porter." I spoke through the green bars.

"I got the same. We'll probably be on the same gang."

"Wonder what it's gonna be like out there, Bayamon? You think maybe like in the movies?"

"Worse, *hermano, mucho* worse," he answered, "'cause this place is the real thing and we ain't no actors."

I grasped the bars of my cell gate firmly and did some light pushaways. "Movies can give you some idea," I said.

"Nay, *papo*," Bayamon countered. "Like you gotta live it. You gotta live it to really know where this place is at.

Coño, I pulled two shorty years my first time and it felt like I was pulling twenty. Coming back on violation is gonna make the three I owe them seem like forever."

"Stop your fucking crying," yelled an unknown voice. "You ain't nothing but a short-timer. I'm pulling thirty to sixty years, motherfucker, and you got the balls to bellyache."

"Fuck you," Bayamon answered without anger. "My three years are as hard to me as your damn sixty are to you."

"Kiss off, faggot," came back the unfriendly voice.

I lit a cigarette, plopped down on my bunk, and settled back to give some deep thought to Bayamon's words. *You gotta live it...you gotta live it...to really know where this place is at.*

The next day we became part of the general prison population. We were marched at breakfast time into a large mess hall where the muffled roar of whispered voices and the sound of metal eating utensils grating against metal plates made a deafening din. There seemed to be over a thousand men in the hall, all dressed in prison gray.

After passing one by one through the food line, we sat down at one of the long metal-top tables. The old-timer inmates stared at us greenhorns and threw in a few unkind remarks for their own pleasure.

"Hey, *hermano*, want your prunes?"

I shook my head no and Bayamon helped himself. "Thanks, man. You'd be surprised how *chévere* prunes are for you. Keep you flushed. Never got to worry about being— what's that *palabra*? Oh, yeah, constipated."

He kept on talking, not caring if I listened or not.

"I once knew a guy that couldn't make a toilet gig for over a week and they hadda rush him to Flower Hospital and put a hose up his *culo*."

A young dark Puerto Rican named Pancho made a face at Bayamon.

"Hey, *por favor*, why don't you cut that conversation out at breakfast?"

Those of us within earshot laughed, a little too loudly. A hack walked over to our table and pointed with a hard-ass reinforced wooden club that I'd learned was called a "nigger stick," supposedly because it could stand against heads that were anything but white.

"Knock it off," the guard said and went back to his position. We knocked it off.

Breakfast over, the different cellblocks began filing out. As our line passed a table with veteran cons still seated, I heard a few indecencies directed at a young kid of about seventeen or eighteen. Reacting like a man, he screamed out angrily in a high-pitched childlike voice.

"You mother sons of bitches try any of your bullshit with me and you're gonna be scraping your fucking guts off the top of your goddamn shoes."

The hack told him to shut up. Our line moved on. None of us could have said it better than the kid. He was almost as skinny as I was. He didn't carry the weight, but he sure carried the heart. We were herded into the large prison yard, there to mingle with hundreds upon hundreds of other cons. I took a deep breath of the hot summer air. All around me were cons, guards, and thirty-foot walls. I walked up and down, my hands shoved deep in my pockets, fingering a pocketful of time.

COMSTOCK WALLS AND GREEN-BARRED STALLS

Sing Sing was a city. It even had sidewalks and lamp-posts. It was also a wealth of bad experiences. No matter how much one hears or reads about prisons, or sees them in films, there is nothing like being a convict. If one has done time before, one knows what to expect, but a first-timer has to learn how to walk a tightrope of safety between bad-ass hacks and uptight fellow cons. You can get wasted by either in no time flat. The guards belt you or worse because they can get away with it. The cons do it out of a sheer sense of angry frustration that is very seldom directed at the hacks and can only be vented with terrible violence at another con.

There are many ways for an inmate to maim or kill another prisoner. In the darkness of a movie, a homemade knife, its handle wrapped in a handkerchief, can be thrust quickly and the weapon tossed away. In the job shops or in the cells, a hand can suddenly fling a can of lye water and cause blindness along with terrible disfiguring burns.

One afternoon I stood near a group of cons in the yard, everything cool and jailhouse normal. Then I noticed an inmate with a tight expression heading slowly toward another inmate who was talking with friends. He began moving faster, and as he passed the talking man, his hand punched out from waist high. He kept on walking as if nothing had happened. The inmate who had been punched in the side merely grunted; his expression was that of annoyance toward a rude person who had bumped him and hadn't apologized. He rubbed his side and continued talking. It wasn't until one of his friends exclaimed, "Hey, man, you're bleeding," that he even realized he had been stabbed. He reported to a guard and simply said he'd been hurt by someone unknown. It was accepted as fact. The wounded inmate would get even his own way.

There was the constant pressure of the asshole artists and their noticeable interest in screwing young cons who had no interest in getting screwed. I remember a nightmare scene I heard from my cell one afternoon when I had joined the early lockup line instead of taking recreation time in the yard.

A sound of scuffling began in the far end of the cellblock. I pressed my ear between the opening of the cell bars and heard the moaning and pleading, the hurt and fright of a young-voiced con being sexually attacked. The grunting violence being forced on that poor kid was clear and unmistakable. I tried to make myself turn off the noise of the unnatural act below, the sounds of flesh being punched, and the cries of forced degradation. I heard a puffing voice say, "Man, he's good." I fought to keep from getting involved, but the kid's pain and shame got to me. Christ, am I the only one who hears the agony going down? Cupping my hands to my mouth and doing my best to disguise my voice, I yelled across the echoing cellblock, "Man in trouble on the flats!"

Some unknown con's voice floated down from another cell, calm and factual: "Whoever you are, you better mind your own business. We hear it, too. Take a tip, buddy. If you can rat on one thing, you can rat on other things, too, and nobody likes a fink, no matter what the reason. Just a fair piece of advice, whoever you are."

I pulled the radio earphones over my ears to get some music going inside my head and muffle the hell that kid was going through. *Nobody from the warden on down gives a damn, as long as it's just cons eating up cons.*

It was not uncommon to hear an inmate standing near one of the lampposts whisper out of the corner of his mouth, "Hey, man, you looking to cop anything? I got phenos, yellow-jackets, reds, some pot, mace and cinnamon." The mace and cinnamon, when taken per spoonful with a glass of hot water, is supposed to produce some kind of high glow. You're supposed to feel stoned.

I would shake my head no because in the first place I was broke. I was smoking Mohawk, prison-issued tobacco with which you roll your own.

"O.K., pal. See me when you get bread. Shit, I'm the best connection in the joint. Keep cool."

I walked to the baseball field fully believing that with his nerve he couldn't help but be the best connection in the joint. Jesus Christ, the cat had probably been a drug-pusher on the outside and here he was busted and taking care of business as usual on the corner of Ossining and Sing Sing.

Sing Sing was in some ways a country club. It was a reception center, serving as a kickoff place for prisoners who stayed only until transferred to other New York State prisons such as Green Haven, Attica, Comstock (Great Meadows), Dannemora (Clinton), and Auburn.

Sing Sing was ideally located, close to New York City, and visitors could come up frequently, the cost to poor families being negligible. It wasn't considered a maximum-security prison and inmates who had served time in other jails swore by the laxity of Sing Sing.

Like, according to the cons, it was easier to get contraband into the place. While other prisons used cigarettes as a means of barter, Sing Sing not only used them, but real folding money floated around to the tune of hundreds of dollars in the pockets or hiding places of many a con. Through the cooperation of a money-hungry guard, you could get a pint of Scotch worth about six bucks on the outside for a paltry thirty or forty bucks inside the walls.

Any convict who managed to pull his time in Sing Sing was said to have good connections on the outside. There were rumors that a big-shot con who belonged to the syndicate had been able to get the wall between his cell and the next knocked down to make one large room, complete with TV, radio, and refrigerator; also that visits were arranged for big-shot inmates with money to spare for a shackup job with some pretty woman in the dead of night. Like all the extra comforts could be gotten if enough money was laid out in the right palms. Mere rumors—but inside it was taken for real. You couldn't tell certain cons apart from the guards because they walked around the prison with the same kind of freedom and type-cast arrogance.

One of my biggest problems was being half-blind without my glasses. The state was taking a helluva time to get me a new pair after my eye test. Why in hell did it take so long to grind a couple of pieces of glass so I could see clearly again? It was bad enough being in prison, but being half-blind was dangerous odds against you.

I approached the baseball field and heard Bayamon call my name. I waved and climbed up into the stands, squinting to make out some faces.

"Hey, fellers. What's happening?" I greeted. I got friendly hellos from Bayamon, Pancho, Gordo, L'il Henry, Bimbo, Zorro, Santurce, and Johnny Lee. Most of us who were together in orientation quarantine had gotten us a clique going. Bayamon had a guitar that had been sent to him and was strumming some home music from Puerto Rico. Pancho and Santurce were rapping out a bongo and conga beat. Zorro was using his comb on the side of a tin can and the rest were clapping hands and stomping feet in perfect Latin rhythm, like Afro-Latin. Gordo was singing a chant, "Hua-huan-co, hua-huan-co." Not to be left out, I made clucking sounds, trying to do a passable impression of *los palitos*, "the little sticks" that are struck together and give an on or off beat. We got the thing going good and more voices joined in to keep up the chant while Gordo took off on some lyrics.

Inmates started grouping around us, out of curiosity or boredom, including the asshole artists. Our newly formed clique stopped chanting and singing and glared as one, and if looks could kill, the asshole artists would have been stripped clean of all flesh. They left, mumbling threats.

Someone started a beat again. Bayamon picked it up on the guitar and once again we jumped into Puerto Rico via El Barrio. Thinking about not ever getting hung up alone at no time, I wished them glasses would come fast. *I got to be able to see clearly more than six or seven feet away. Ain't no good having to wait till those* maricones *are right on top of you.* I went back to making clucking sounds in time to the music.

One October afternoon a couple of months later, I was on my mopping detail when a guard approached me and said, "Come with me. You're keep-locked." I asked him what for. He just beckoned me with his night stick, so I let the mop lean against the wall and followed him. I was locked up, and a sign was placed on my bars: KEEP LOCK.

"Will you tell me what the keep-lock is for?" I asked again.

"You're on a shipment to Comstock, Great Meadows Correctional Institution. You'll be up at 4:00 A.M. tomorrow morning. Get your personal things together."

A con's voice trailed toward my cell.

"Hey, you're going to Comstock?"

"That's what the man said," I replied.

"Shit, buddy. That's a maximum-security prison."

It don't sound like that, I thought. It's a correctional institution. I left the thought up in the air. It couldn't be worse than this joint...or could it?

Next morning at 4:00 A.M. about thirty of us inmates were taken to the mess hall for an early breakfast. I noticed that most of the guys I had formed friendships with were on the shipment with me, including Pancho, Zorro, and Bayamon. After breakfast, we were handcuffed in couples and our ankles shackled, Pancho's right side to my left. We were loaded into a prison train and headed for the Great Meadows Correctional Institution at Comstock, New York, better known simply as "Comstock."

I squinted through the dusty train window and watched the blurry snow-covered scenes go rattling by. I tried to get as comfortable as possible, but it wasn't easy with my leg irons attached to Pancho. I tugged at them to make my foot comfortable. Pancho woke up and smiled.

"If you can find the key to these fucking irons, I'll give

you all the room you want, *hermano*."

The train rickety-racked its way to a place that was gonna be my home for maybe up to fifteen years.

"Ever been to Comstock prison, Pancho?" I spoke to the window.

"*Nunca, hombre,* but I'm sure of what's there."

"Yeah, like what?"

"Like more of what we just left behind, except that where we're going it's maximum security. The hacks are supposed to have eyes in their assholes."

"*Oye,* any of you *compadres* like an extra cheese sandwich?" offered Bayamon, who was seated behind us. Pancho shook his head no. I did the same.

"Stop worrying, you guys." Bayamon gave out some comforting words. "You'll survive in the new place. All you got to do is belong to a clique. Like, one for all and all for one."

"What are you? One of the three musketeers?" joked Pancho. "Sounds like a good idea, but from past experience, when the shit goes down you're usually fighting alone.

Bayamon swallowed the last of his dry cheese sandwich and countered with, "Yeah, maybe, but being part of a clique is better than walking alone. Besides, if you follow a few basic rules, you gotta better chance of making it."

"Like what?" I asked.

"Like make believe you trust everybody, but don't trust nobody. Like don't take loans or presents from stranger cons. It may be part of a game to get you in debt and collect from your *culo* with a one-thousand percent interest."

"Yeah, man," Pancho broke in. "Listen lots and talk little."

"You better believe it," said Bayamon, checking out some cheese between his teeth. "At the first sign of shit coming your way from a con, bust him in the mouth. Better to win or lose fighting than cop out and earn a punko rep."

"If you got heart, the word gets around. If you ain't, that gets around even faster."

"That's the way anywhere," I grunted.

"More so inside the joint, *amigo*," Bayamon smiled.

"It's a damn good rule," I agreed.

Better get myself back into shape, I thought. Pushups, lifting weights, 'cause Charles Atlas never got nowhere as a ninety-seven-pound weakling.

"Another thing a con better learn. Like if he's gotta gamble, he better gamble with what he's got, not with what he's gonna get. 'Cause if he loses and can't pay, shame on him. Welshers got a hard way to go."

I grinned at Bayamon and said, "You're a regular book on survival, ain't you?"

"You better be, too, *panín*. Grow eyes in the back of your head and make an ear out of every pore of your body. And along with that, get yourself some kind of weapon, like a small piece of steel bar to hold in your fist for added punch power or more than one homemade shive, like hide blades around in different places. In case the hacks find one, you still got reserves."

The pounding motion of the train made me groggy. I was half-asleep for some time, barely hearing Bayamon talk. I woke up straight when Pancho nudged me and said, "Diggit, there's our new *casa*."

I pressed up against the train window and dug that Comstock was smaller-looking than Sing Sing. It was down in a valley with so many acres and acres of cleared land around it that the nearest wooded area seemed a thousand miles away.

Seeing what looked like a graveyard outside the prison walls, we cons couldn't help making comments about it. Instead of crosses or tombstones, each grave had a slab of white-painted wood above it. A veteran convict explained that it was boot hill for convicts who had made free side through the backdoor, like in death they got freedom. "That marker above each grave has the number of the dead man painted on it instead of his name," he said.

Jesus Christ, the goddamn prison could at least have given the dead their names back. I began repeating my name over and over in my head. I wasn't ever gonna forget it, no matter how many damn numbers they painted over me.

The train stopped and we were taken off. The icy air froze

us while the snow crunched most unfriendly under our prison clodhopper boots.

A short while later we were standing in a large room in Great Meadows Correctional Institution. Our cuffs and shackles were removed and we went through a processing similar to Sing Sing's. We were in quarantine about ten days or so, during which I got permission to see the eye doctor. I was developing eye strain from trying to see through the blur of my near-sighted eyes. I explained that my eyes had been examined in Sing Sing and asked if my glasses had been transferred here to Comstock along with me.

The doctor checked through a pile of eyeglass cases and came up with a pair that had my number on it. They had a yellow plastic frame. I put them on and it was as if someone had lit the sun up for me. It wasn't blurred night any longer. I could see clearly and felt confidence rush to my heart. Man, I would be able to see a friend or foe clearly at least a block away.

I guarded them well. When I was asleep, they were always in their metal case under my pillow; awake, they were over my eyes. They were just a pair of ordinary thick-lensed eyeglasses in a cheap plastic frame, but to me they represented confidence and *mucho* more odds in my favor. In the world of those who could see clearly, I was an equal again. I didn't have to depend on nobody's eyes but my own.

I thought of my new prison number—18193. I repeated it over and over. We had been warned by a hack to memorize our numbers like we didn't have names while guests of the state. 18193...18193...18193, I repeated it softly. *Hell,* I murmured, *numba 18193 ain't me.*

Now I Lay Me Down to Time

Every day at Great Meadows Correctional Institution was the same. Our lives were regulated by the sound of a trumpet. It blared at 7:30 A.M. every morning to get us up for breakfast and work. It blared again at 12:00 noon for lunch, and at 3:30 P.M. it signaled the end of the workday and time for supper. There was also yard recreation, and then around 5:00 P.M. it sounded for lock-in time. We remained in our cells from fourteen to sixteen hours to await another day of the trumpet.

Saturdays and Sundays we were off and had yard privileges most of the day, until 5:00 P.M. In summertime, we had movies on Sunday; in wintertime, we had them on Saturday and Sunday. You could either go to the movies, stay in the yard, or keep to your cell. You couldn't go home.

Like in Sing Sing, I had been assigned to the mop gang. I wondered if the only way I was ever going to work my way up from the mop gang was to work my way up to the end of my mop stick and sit on it.

There was a guard I nicknamed "Siegfried the Hack" because he walked around the prison with the attitude of a World War II Nazi, and every time he looked at me it was as if I were Jewish. He was a damn big man of about 220 pounds of solid muscle, and he had a reputation of trying to show what a fair-minded guard he was by offering a bare-fisted fight with any con who wanted or dared to take him on. He always ended the offer with the same words, "It'll be a fair fight. We'll go to the back of the shop and get to it. If you win, nothing will be said. If I win, the same."

But everyone knew it was bullshit, especially a few trust-ing brave-hearted inmates who had foolishly taken him on and won—'cause the next thing they knew they were getting their behinds whipped on some trumped-up pretext, never for whipping Siegfried, always for something else.

One day he was laying the same old bull-crap line on a group of us. I must have stared at him a little too long and he read some kind of contempt on my face because he straight-way offered me a shot at his title. I just smiled faintly and grimly shook my head in a No-thank-you-Mr.-John-Sullivan.

"Don't you believe me about it being a fair one?" He was glaring at me.

"All the way," I answered, and finished the thought in my mind, "all the way up to my going to the hospital."

"Well, then?" Siegfried pushed his superiority at me.

I let my voice come out calm and answered, "I'd be a fool to go up against you knowing you're damn good with your fists," and added mentally, "and your goon squad complete with nigger sticks." I smiled disarmingly and eased out of the pressure by adding, "Naw, you're the champ." All around me I could sense my rapport with the fellow cons as I played a dangerous game. They all knew where Siegfried was at and hated his guts. Siegfried pushed at me.

"What'sa matter? Ain't got guts? You're one of them cop-shooters, ain't you? Name and picture in the papers. I read about you. Tough little nigger, ain't you?"

My mind couldn't help going back to the Tombs and remembering what the former prizefighter named Tank had told me about guards in prison being extra heavy on cons who had been involved in cop-shootings.

My next move toward survival was not answering back, thereby giving Siegfried his opening toward fearlessly plant-ing bumps on my head, not only for his benefit but also for my fellow inmates. It worked both ways. Siegfried glared at me and growled something about, "You better walk between the raindrops from now on 'cause I'll be watching real close, and the first time you get wet in some infraction of prison rules, I'll be there to lay it on nice and heavy. You'd have been shit without a gun." And emitting a whole lot of hate, he walked away.

I let the words slide out softly, "...And you'd be less than shit without your goddamn nigger stick and goon squad to back you up."

As I watched his retreating back, I made a very important mental note to stay out of Siegfried's violent way. He was like a lot of guards who would goad a con into reacting in blind fury in order to have an excuse to wet the earth with his blood. Since cons were a danger too, sometimes even more so, part of surviving was to learn how to build an invisible cocoon around oneself, a force field against anyone getting too close. Guard or con, someone you're buddy-buddy with might turn out to be today's *amigo* and *mañana's* enemy.

If you have no one sending you money or food packages from the outside, then you have to hustle. If your hustling is not successful, then you've got to replenish the larder in your cell somehow because when hunger hits you somewhere in the night, there's no delicatessen from which to order corned beef sandwiches.

Those of us who were welfare cases according to the prison system, would smuggle sandwiches made up of whatever was in the mess hall. Sometimes the sandwiches would be made up of beans, sometimes baloney, macaroni, spaghetti, and even of soup with two slices of bread dipped in it and embellished with thin noodles and a shadow of meat.

Smuggling food was against the prison rules because it was alleged that food taken to the cells would bring on an invasion of mice and roaches. But there was no rule against eating the mice and roaches if you were hungry enough. Prison food did not have staying power. Those of us who worked hard needed something more substantial than a high starch diet.

I used to kick myself mentally in my cell many times when I was hungry for not having listened to my mother as a kid and cleaned my plate at breakfast, lunch or supper. My taste buds could actually taste the long-past wasted food and I'd go to sleep with a grumbling stomach, envisioning huge steaks with hundred-course trimmings.

There was no doubt that inmates of white ethnic extraction seemed always to have the better deals in prison. I remember once being assigned to paint inside the warehouse where food stockpiles were kept. It was a huge place with all kinds of canned goods and produce. The inmate trustees working there were Italians. One of them was talking about Lucky Luciano, who had been an inmate here until he had made a deal with the United States Government to return to Italy and organize the partisans during World War II in exchange for his freedom. It sounded like something out of the movies. The conversation had more than a hint that a lot of syndicate money had passed into hot hands as part of the deal. It was also said that just before Luciano was to be released he had wanted to donate $100,000 to the prison for a gymnasium. The offer was turned down by the warden, though a gym was something the state should have built long ago. Rehabilitation needs healthy bodies as well as healthy minds.

I watched the Italian inmates cooking spaghetti. The warehouse was filled with the savory aroma of clam sauce, oregano, and garlic, and I couldn't stop my taste buds from going haywire. A flood of water filled my mouth as my nose drank in the richness of the sauce and spaghetti. I didn't look their way dead on, just a glance from time to time. Damn, I envied them their connections, their money and power, which reached even into the prison yards.

"Hey, kid," the Italian who was cooking called out to me. I looked at him—only the gray hairs at his temples stopped him from being twenty-five instead of the forty he must have been. Good living inside the walls kept him healthy and strong.

"Yeah?" I answered.

"Wanna drop that paint brush? We got plenty. Wanna eat?"

Damn, I sure do. Christ Almighty! It's been a long time

since I had some Italian cooking and here it is—white clam sauce, garlic, chickpeas, and spaghetti al dente.

I opened my mouth with good intentions, but what came out was, "Naw, thanks, but I ain't hungry."

"Suit yourself, buddy." And forgetting about me, he served his *amigos*.

I watched them eating as if at a banquet. I wondered why I hadn't accepted. Maybe he had wanted something in return that I couldn't give, or maybe to lord it over me, or maybe he had simply felt sorry for me. Whatever the reason was, I was glad I had refused. I wouldn't have enjoyed it because I envied their advantageous prison connections. I tried to tune down the overpowering smell of Italian cooking by thinking of the Puerto Rican food at home, but no good. My kind of food was nowhere in sight. The spaghetti in clam sauce was here and now. I just inhaled the smell of fresh green paint a little deeper than usual in a last act of defiance while a little voice in my stomach said, *Asshole. You shouldda copped some of that great spaghetti. What are you? Some kind of nut or something?* I didn't answer.

The trustees went about their business with a freedom that was second only to the guards'. They were permitted to go almost anywhere in the prison they wanted, with passes, of course. They were the prisoners' main source of communication. The trustees who worked in the front office got the word on anything good or bad that was to happen and spread it to the rest of us. If there was going to be a search of our cells for weapons' contraband, we'd know about it. If a V.I.P. was coming to tour the prison, we'd know it. Trustees were the lifeline of the prison grapevine. They could also be stoolies, but if they were informers, they lived dangerously. The same grapevine could expose them.

They were able to work outside the prison walls and were always in a better position to wheel and deal in procuring fresh milk, eggs, and meat, and in selling their wares to non-trustees.

To be a trusty, one had to have a good prison record, a nonviolent criminal record, a short sentence, and no warrants awaiting one on release. The list of requirements left me out of the running completely. My crime had been violent, my time was long, and I had two warrants awaiting me. Plus, I had been sentenced to hard labor.

Had some miracle made me a trusty outside the walls, I used to wonder if I would without hesitation look for another miracle and find myself across the border in Canada or Mexico. I didn't feel guilty about doing a running act if I made trusty. I'd have been crazy to dig prison, and, besides, those armed robbery warrants I was facing were loaded with more prison time. I went back to painting, comforting myself with *You can't have everything. Damn shame, though. A trustee's got it made.*

Pancho, Bayamon, and I were on a mop gang, spaced out about six feet apart. I started off first, waltzing backward with a soapy mop, Pancho came next with a rinse mop, and Bayamon followed through with a dry mop.

The three of us moving in syncopated rhythm made it look like a ballet. We had the mop technique down to an effortless science.

I broke out laughing when Bayamon began putting on a mambo contest with his mop, throwing the mop handle out, doing some fancy dance steps, spinning around, and catching the handle before it hit the cement floor. But the enjoyment went out the window as Siegfried came in on the scene. He always stood like some general reviewing his troops, and now his tongue blasted at Bayamon through the cellblock, "If you got so much damn talent, why the hell aren't you in show business instead of pushing a mop in here?"

Bayamon straightened out, got serious, and let us know he was about to bullshit. His voice took on the proper note of humility.

"That's why I'm practicing, sir. So when I get out, my name can go up in lights. I wanna make it real big, sir, so I'll never have to come to a terrible place like this again."

"You getting wise with me, feller?"

"Not at all, sir." Bayamon's voice preserved the delicate

balance. "I'm very serious about getting to be a big star. I want to prove I'm taking advantage of being re-ha-bil-tated. Anybody that stays in this place ain't got no good sense or can't make it anyplace else."

Pancho and I strained not to burst a gut laughing. Bayamon's last sentence had gone over his head. Siegfried the Hack put his full attention to us for the first time as he noticed us resting on our mop handles, legs crossed. He bellowed, "Lean, dammit, lean on them damn mops. Move it, move it."

He went back to his observation spot at the end of the block and glared at us from time to time. As soon as he turned his attention elsewhere, Bayamon threw the most *chévere* dance steps, spun twice this time, and still caught the mop handle before it hit the floor. If he had missed, Siegfried would have had an excuse to take care of head-pounding business with him.

We finished to the end of the cellblock and I put out my hand, signaling for a five-minute break for smoking time. Siegfried waved his club in a begrudging O.K. I started to roll a cigarette, but Pancho offered me a tailor-made. I took it and smiled thanks.

"Man, like this job is for the birds," I said. "I'm getting rehabilitated for the wrong vocation, 'cause I sure as hell ain't gonna push no mop when and if I ever get out."

"It's better than some other of them jobs, like digging ditches or unplugging shit holes," Pancho grinned.

"Maybe mopping is your bag, Pancho, but like I've had it. Shit, man. I even dug myself mopping in my dreams."

"So put in a tab for a job change," Bayamon suggested.

"I already did, man."

"Where to?" Pancho asked.

"Mess hall."

"Uh-uh. You ought to know better. That's for *blanquitos*. Only P.R.'s or colored guys are pushing mop or are on the garbage detail. Check it out, *papo*."

"Anyway, the second choice is for sick bay."

"Check that out, too, *amigo*. Same entrance requirements: *blanco-americano*." Pancho was such a damn wealth of information.

"The third is for the paint gang and the last is for the library. I put it last 'cause I figure you don't get what you ask for first."

You gotta be kidding, *hombre*. They give them jobs to the old-timers or the young-timers with good education and the same old color."

"Yeah, I know," I shrugged. "But at least trying beats a blank. Who knows, there might be a chance."

Pancho smiled and said, "Yeah, same chance an elephant would have trying to screw a flea."

We all laughed. Two weeks later I was assigned to the paint gang, and Pancho and Bayamon got transferred too, and without even asking for it. My new apartment was C-5-13 (the *C* meant C-Block).

I painted bars, cells, and beds. I got to hate the colors green, buff, and white. I reached the point where I would paint automatically and blot out whatever was being painted. My fingers were sticky with green paint and I couldn't help thinking I not only had to look through those bars all the damn time, I also had to make them look pretty with that crappy green paint.

Not all my time was spent working. I was attending classes—taking mechanical drawing, drafting, and brick masonry. My courses were staggered so that some days I'd work in the morning and go to school in the afternoon, and vice versa.

I had also been busy getting my high-school diploma. When the guard propped a large envelope between the bars of my cell, I felt a sense of pride. In the envelope was a diploma issued in my name. It didn't say "Great Meadows Correctional Institution" at the top. Instead, it read "State University of New York."

I smiled to myself remembering the time I had learned my mark was 283 (all that was needed to pass was 225). I had let my voice reverberate through the cellblock toward Zorro, who had also taken the high school equivalency test.

"Zorro—hey—Zorro!"

"Yeah, *panín*, what's happening?"

"Diggit. I'm a genius. I passed with 283. How about that shit, huh?"

"Not bad, *panín*, not bad at all." He crushed my ego by adding, "I made a mark of 298. But don't let it get you down. Keep punching."

I had comforted myself by yelling back a good-natured praise. "Goddamn smart-ass."

These accomplishments were achieved under difficult circumstances because the constant threats and violence of prison were a twenty-four hour menace. You had to create a dimension of your own and shut out the hell-filled hours in order to concentrate on your studies. Half your mind was on your classwork and the other half was checking out whatever looked like a possibility of harm coming your way from any direction.

There were facilities for courses in sheet-metal working, machine shop, carpentry, and brick masonry, as well as academic classes, but the most that could be packed into the small classrooms were twenty to thirty men a day, and there were around fourteen hundred inmates in the place. It was like trying to educate a cup of coffee with a drop of milk.

Some inmates took correspondence courses for college credit. Others took advanced courses in architecture, refrigeration, even TV. But it was all theory. There really wasn't the physical plant in Great Meadows for the all-important phase of learning—practical experience.

We blacks and Puerto Ricans in prison took our courses and studied our brains out, but without much hope of ever really working at the trade outside 'cause we knew from past experience that the high-paying trade jobs were monopolized by unions that were bigot-controlled and would now keep the door locked to us for two reasons instead of one. We were the wrong-colored race, and now we were also ex-cons.

But taking courses gave our minds something to dwell upon besides the walls. Otherwise, there was nothing but dead time in a dead end. If out of the two or three civilian teachers in the place, one wasn't half-indifferent, it counted for something. The consensus among the prisoners was that they, too, were frustrated by the poorly equipped shop and classrooms and by the pressure put on them to perform miracles with practically nothing except the terrible need of our minds to learn some academic or vocational trade, though we might never be given a chance to use it on free side.

But we resented their indifference and felt they were only there to collect a paycheck. It was a laugh to watch them making out fabulous reports on our progress. Once when I had built the facade of a brick country house complete with windows and a stoop as well as a combination outdoor fireplace, oven, and barbecue pit, pictures were taken by the officials. Some weeks later, the pictures had been shown in a nearby country fair along with other works of convicts' arts and crafts. I was told that my entry of bricks held together with clay had won some sort of ribbon or honorable mention. Nobody handed me a ribbon, so I figured it had been pinned on the school supervisor. I shook my head and thought, *Rehabilitation, my ass*. It was nothing but a game to make people outside think we were being molded into productive human beings. We were being taught, all right, taught how to feel less than human. Every time we were called by a number instead of a name, we were dehumanized.

I walked toward the warden's office, a sergeant by my side. Bayamon, who was passing by, looked askance at me and mouthed the words, "Are you in trouble?"

"Uh-uh, just trying to get permission to write to my girl Trina."

Bayamon made a good-luck gesture. I passed through a lot of gates and finally stood in front of the warden's desk. He had my letter in front of him, plus what I was sure was my file. He studied what was there for a while and finally looked up at me. I stood at ease with my hands clasped behind my back.

"Cross your elbows, chest high!" the sergeant ordered. I folded my arms and waited for the warden to speak first. One of the million rules in prison is you ask for permission to speak or wait until you are spoken to.

"I see you are requesting permission to write to a person named Trina."

"Yes, sir."

"I see you say she is your girl."

"Yes, sir. I hope to marry her when I get out."

"And who is this Lucien you have on your mailing list?"

"Lucien, sir, is a girl who gave birth to my son and got on my mailing list as my common-law wife. I guess she figured I could support the kid even though I was in here."

"And you don't want to write to her?"

"I don't love her, sir. It was one of those things that happen. We just met and dug each other for the moment. Besides, she doesn't write to me except for one time, to ask for money, and what can I give her out of the nickel a day I'm making? If I could help her and the baby, I would. But, like Trina's my real girl."

The warden looked hard at me. His mouth got a little tight, then he let it stream out.

"What the hell do you think you're running, a harem? Permission denied. Wait till you get back outside to take care of whatever."

I muscled myself for control and told myself, *Don't beg, Piri, don't beg*, and my voice came out cool.

"Sir, you don't understand. There wasn't anything real between me and Lucien. We dug each other that one time. She might have feeling for me, I don't know, but I do know I love Trina and it would mean a lot to me to be able to correspond with her. I'm really sure she would like to also. How about it, sir?"

"You just wait till you get out to take care of your personal harem."

"Sir, I ain't asking for all that much. I'd—"

The Sergeant's hand tightened on my shoulder and turned it firmly toward the door. The interview was over. I looked at the warden and took the risk—my voice had to carry sarcasm thinly veiled in courtesy.

"Thank you very much for your consideration of my

request."

If the warden dug my sarcasm he didn't let on. He just said, "Thank you, what?"

I smiled gently and whispered, "Thank you, *sir*."

I walked out into the prison yard wondering what kind of a cat could be so rotten to the feelings of a guy who just wanted to write his girl. What fucking right did he have to moralize and judge me as to my loving and being loved, regardless of the depth or scope? Love is love whether for a moment or all of eternity. What right did he have? And I answered myself. *All the right in the world, baby. Ain't he God in the Divine Person of the Warden?*

Christ, if I'd've been him, I'da said, "Sure, go ahead, feller. Write to your girl. Man, like love is a beautiful thing. It's part of your rehabilitation. Like, if you let enough love into your life, there ain't no room for hate. In fact, why don't you ask her to visit you? You got my permission for as many times as she wants to come and visit. We want you to go out into that world loving, not hating."

I smiled at my mental bullshitting.

"How'd you make out?" Bayamon checked me out.

"I got struck out on the first swing. Fuck it! That's just the way the ball bounces."

But inside of me I was saying, *Shit! It would have meant so much to me. Add one more little pound of hate.*

To keep from being molded completely into a gray-clothed, numbered robot, I constantly fought institutionalization. Because once you came through those huge green gates of no hope, the process of breaking you down as a thinking individual began with a constant, daily, staccato-like bombardment of "Talk," "Don't Talk," "Walk," "Don't Walk," "Eat," "Don't Eat," "Sleep," "Don't Sleep," "Sick," "Not Sick." Yard time—cell time—discipline time—punishment time—insult time—cracked-head and sudden-death time.

A group of us were gathered one day around a championship game of horseshoes, and betting was heavy in terms of cigarettes. I heard a commotion and, looking around, saw a

Puerto Rican named Eddie Lopez making his way toward us at a fast clip. His face had excitement written on it, his body was damn near jumping with strange joy.

"Hey, fellers. I'm back. Je-sus Christ, how you guys been? I really missed your ugly faces."

We all greeted him. I smiled at him and shook hands.

"Damn, man. Like old times. What's been happening since I left? Christ, I'm glad to see you cats again."

Holy Christ! So that's being institutionalized. The system had molded him to the point where he missed "home sweet prison." He was glad to be back. He was home with his familiar buddy-con faces, his father images in the persons of both hacks and cons. Home where his brothers were. He was back where he didn't have to worry about looking for a job or hassling income tax forms, where he didn't have to compete to the extent demanded on the outside. He was home where he would be fed, clothed, and watched over, where he wouldn't have to make any real decisions. Home again!

"What's shaking on the outside, Eddie?" I asked.

And Eddie López poured out a torrent of words describing what was happening on the streets where he had felt so damn lonely and homesick.

Man, I thought, staring at him, *that's institutionalized.*

HAIR IS HAIR, AIN'T IT?

I hadn't had a haircut since Sing Sing and my guard now ordered me to get one. I went to the barbershop with a line of other cons, saw an empty chair, and sat in it.

"Gimme a short trim," I mumbled and waited for the barber to put the sheet round my neck. Nothing happened. I turned around and my eyes got stuck to a white inmate who was just staring at me. I looked at him casually and dug he was not a guard because he had on a gray uniform like mine with convict smelling all over it.

"I said gimme a short trim," I repeated and turned away. I waited for the sheet to be fitted round my neck.

"Can't cut your hair," I heard a weak voice say.

"Not too much off the top—hey, what did you say?" I swiveled around in the barber chair. My eyes got mean, his got even meaner.

"I said I can't cut your hair."

"And why the hell can't you? You ain't crippled, I notice. Or is it because you ain't no fuckin' barber?"

"I'm a barber, but I still can't cut your hair. I got my orders."

Our conversation up to now was almost whispered.

"What do you mean you can't cut my hair? I got bugs or something?"

"Look, I'm sorry if your feelings are hurt, but these scissors are for cutting a white man's hair only. Your kind of hair is too tough. It dulls the scissors and ruins them for white hair."

"Whew!" I'd heard it but I couldn't believe it. This cat meant it. He had orders, but like from whom? Other white convicts?

"You'd better cut my hair." I looked at his scissors and he saw where my mind was at if I grabbed them from him. He pulled back about three feet and yelled, "I don't want no trouble but I ain't suppose to cut your hair."

He said it loud and clear for a good reason, because it brought him help in the form of two guards who looked at me pleasantly. One said to the barber, "Any trouble, feller?"

"I ain't suppose to cut his hair."

"Hair is hair, ain't it?" I shot back at him.

"You shouldn't be upset, feller," the other guard said to me. I watched his hand tightly wrap the leather thong on his night stick.

"You got enough of your own barbers to take care of your hair, haven't you?"

"This cat's a con just like me," I said, feeling stupid because I knew damn well no amount of gray uniform was gonna stop him from being white and no amount of gray uniform was gonna make me white.

"Now, do you want a haircut or something else done to your head?"

I looked around that barbershop and black, brown, and white faces were digging the scene. I was all alone. I took a deep breath, chewed hard at the pride in my guts, eased off the barber chair. Forcing a tight smile, I said to the guard, "I'll just take a haircut, if you don't mind."

"That's a good boy," said one guard. "You'll never have no sweat if you just do as you're told."

I moved past them, stopping an instant enough to let the racist con know the love in my heart for him was waiting to show itself someday in some private alley.

I got my haircut from a black Puerto Rican who kept saying, "You did right, backing off. Yes, sir, odds were too damn much against you."

After his fourth or fifth, "Yes, sir, odds were too damn much against you," I squeezed some anger at him through my clenched teeth, "Hey, man, just gimme a fuckin' haircut and never mind the lip."

He wasn't expecting that, and in the wall mirror I saw his face take on a surprised, almost hurt look. Then he started to get uptight. I shook my head and forced a tight smile at him, whispering, "Sorry, *amigo*. I'm taking out my heat on you. That ain't right."

"No sweat, pal." He grinned and took off on my black man's hair with gusto.

After he finished, I started back to my job, but at the door as I fumbled in my pockets for the ever necessary pass that would get me safely through the army of guards, I swore I heard someone say, "That's a smart-ass nigger." Anger got the best of me, and I turned around to look at the guards and at the white convict barber. No one said anything. The guards just stared hard at me and the con barber let a shy, knowing grin wash over his face. I turned and walked slowly out the door, then stood in the yard, feeling the hot steam blowing inside of me.

Christ! I felt so goddamn helpless. I could almost hear the Puerto Rican's comforting words, "Yes, sir, odds were too damn much against you." I made my way across the yard.

I saw the principal keeper, a thin old man who was sort of a general manager, and approached him.

"I'd like to talk to you for a second."

He stared at me and waited. I added the forced "sir" that was always demanded.

"Yes, what is it?"

I chose my words carefully. I explained to him about going for a haircut and what had gone down with the scissors that could only cut a white man's hair and were ruined if they touched a non-white head.

Without a trace of emotion, he simply said, "That's true... that's why you have your own barbers. Anything else?"

I nodded no.

"Go on about your business."

I started to walk away.

"What's your number?"

"18193." I looked at him.

"18193, what?"

"18193, *sir.*"

He nodded and dismissed me with a flick of his forefinger. I walked on in the big yard. I had known better but had wanted to make sure where the white barber's orders had come from. I went to the handball court, got into a fast game, and took out my anger on a little red Spalding ball.

No matter how hard I slammed that damn ball, I couldn't get rid of the anger. Bigotry was bad enough on the outside. I could sometimes walk away from it just by being alone with my girl, but inside this damn place, it was a blanket that kept me constantly wrapped up in a controlled atmosphere of racism. The damn prison system played pocket pool with our balls by having the white guards encourage the white cons to feel superior to nonwhites.

A month later, haircut day rolled around again. I got a pass from my shop guard and headed to the barbershop. A few inmate barbers, both black and white, were outside getting some air while awaiting customers. The guards were inside. One of the cons was the white-man's-hair barber. Our eyes locked. A little smile broke the corner of his thin-lipped mouth. My face grew tight and my jaws clenched. I could hear my teeth grinding against each other as some kind of energy began to flow between us, vibrating in hatred.

He had smiled his put-down at me so it was up to me to answer in kind. I flipped out what I thought would bug him the most.

"What you smiling about, you goddamn white nigger?" I spoke in a low voice.

"What, what did you say?" His whole body jerked up stiff.

Again softly, "You heard me, nigger. I know you got neegro blood in you from the git-go. That's why you came down so hard on me last time. You want to cover up that your Mammy's black."

His face got bright red and he started to open his mouth to say something. I cut him off. "Let's go behind the barbershop, cool-like, so the hacks don't take notice—that is, if you got heart, faggot."

We stood there a moment, silently killing each other with

looks, while the other cons stared at both of us—mostly at him, though, to see if he was going to cop out. I kept hoping he wouldn't take up the challenge and thus really screw up his prison rep by branding himself a coward. I could sense his mind going a mile a minute, weighing the situation. The faces of the white cons were dead on him, like promising him an ass-whipping if he let the white prison population down by copping out to me. He knew it so shrugging his shoulders very cool, he said to no one in particular, "Give a whistle if the hack starts coming around the back."

The two of us started for the back of the barbershop. He didn't trust me and I didn't trust him, so we walked with at least four feet between us. Once in the back, we faced each other. I let my heavy gray prison jacket slip off. He left his on and smiled. I dug instantly why he had done so—the material was heavy wool and would act as a cushion against body blows. I didn't give a crap about his strategy. I could move faster without mine, and besides, it wasn't his body I wanted to hit. It was his smiling mouth I wanted to smash.

Christ! Hate was emanating from both of us and it made the air crackle.

He put up his hands and went into a semi-low crouch, smiling that shit grin, and said softly, "Deal, *nigger*."

He must have expected me to start dancing around, jabbing, hooking, and all the rest of that bullshit, because he wasn't prepared when I let out some kind of pent-up growl and charged him, slamming lefts and rights into his face. He fell up against a bush next to the wall and toppled over it, then rolled over and over on the ground till he was far enough from me to get up safely. He probably figured I was going to stomp his guts in if I caught him on the ground, and the S.O.B. was right. There wasn't any Marquis of Queensberry rules applying here. He'd do the same to me. I swung a right at his head, connected and felt my knuckles scream out in pain as my ribs got pounded by his fists. We just kept at it, swinging, hitting, missing, getting hit, no words, no curses, only deadly hate.

Light flashed in front of my eyes as I got a roundhouse on

the side of my head. We closed in on each other and locked, wrestling for time to rest, for time to catch the other off guard. Our faces were no more than two inches apart. In our urge to obliterate each other, we were like the last two men on earth fighting for supremacy over an empty world.

I felt, rather than saw, his knee coming up at my groin and had a split second to snap my legs together to keep myself from getting crippled. There ain't nobody ever walked away with smashed testicles. He missed my groin. The knee caught me on the inside of my right thigh, but the force was enough to make me grunt in pain. Inside my head I kept repeating he wasn't going to beat me. I was going to beat him, 'cause he had gotten me to hate him more than he could ever hate me. I grabbed at him and came away with my left hand full of his long hair—with his head and body still attached to it. He stumbled off balance and I swung my right fist from way behind my shoulder into his face again and again. I was drunk on hate. I let out all the frustration, anger, and bitterness of my blackness. I battered him as if he alone was responsible for my being in prison, my being from a ghetto, my being born poor, down, and brown.

Suddenly I felt an arm around my throat and a hand pulling at my arms. I knew I was about to die from a skull crushed by some guard's handmade, hand-named nigger stick. I didn't give a damn. I couldn't see too well with the hot salty sweat on my head rolling into my eyes and mixing with even hotter and saltier tears of rage. I didn't struggle. I was spent. My jacket was handed to me. I put it on and slipped my glasses on a swollen nose. My vision became clearer. There were no guards. My nose dripped needles of red. I remembered him hitting me only twice. Where did the other hurts come from?

All around me were black and Puerto Rican cons. Around my opponent, who was crouched against the wall, were white cons. We glared at each other. Nothing was said. It was very quiet behind the barbershop, and I felt calm inside me. The lightning had gone and the thunder had stopped.

I heard a voice tinged with a Puerto Rican accent, "The

odds were better this time, eh, *amigo*? You better forget your
hair this time, 'cause your face don't look so good."

I didn't answer. I just nodded, and without looking back
at anything except my victory, I walked away cleaning my
face and feeling satisfied. There were no reprisals, no busts
from the guards, no solitary confinement, *nada*. What had
gone down between El Blanco and me wasn't the guards'
business. It was ours.

Most of us inmates were between twenty and thirty-five
years old and full of vim and vigor. We strove mightily to
work off our excess energies by playing handball, baseball,
football, and by taking up the still more strenuous pastime of
weight lifting. Weights weren't easy to come by in prison and
ordering them from the outside cost a bundle of money.

So we made our own simply by getting two empty five-
gallon paint cans, filling them with borrowed cement, and
joining them with a four-foot iron bar from the plumbing
shop, also borrowed. We would have a weight of over a hundred pounds. If we couldn't get a metal bar for the grip, we'd
make one out of wood. But that was dangerous, for if it broke
while you were doing a press, you could suffer a painful
injury.

When the weather was bad, we had the choice of staying
in our cells or going to the recreation hall. But the "recreation" was in name only. The hall had nothing except a shuf-
fleboard painted on the smooth cement floor, green metal
tables, and benches. It was a large hall, freezing in wintertime and muggy and damp when it rained.

The recreation consisted of checkers, chess, dirty hearts,
whist, bridge, seven-card rummy, five-hundred rummy, and
every kind of poker and blackjack you could name.

If you had tailor-mades, you could gamble. Otherwise, the
cheapest form of recreation was just plain old bullshitting,
and gossiping about anything or anybody. Topics ranged from
sex, art, sex, philosophy, sex, and life in general to conditions
in prison, sex, politics, sex, and drugs, and on to used, reused,
overused, and abused master plans for breaking out of the

goddamn place. And without much hope of it ever happening, we could sit around and wish the seven plagues that fell on Biblical Egypt would strike the official prison ruling class, from the warden on down. But if one was tired of all the bullshit, one could always sit alone in some corner, turn into one's mind, and think positive or brood negative. It was the last stronghold of privacy.

Sport substitution helped me work off prison pressure, but when lockup time rolled around and the next fourteen to sixteen hours were to be spent in a cell, even dynamic tension got tiring. Dynamic tension is the science of building muscles without weights, simply by using the pressure and strain of one part of your body against another, and doing breathing exercises. But how long can one stay interested in doing pushups, even one on hand?

The radio we got in our cells by plugging earphones into a wall socket always had the same station on the air. It seemed whoever worked the dial in the communication room knew only one station.

I started to sketch and draw pictures, first with an ordinary pencil. As I got into it, I began to deal with pastels, but I could only do so much of that before it was a bore. Moreover, there wasn't a limitless supply of chalks and paper, and if you couldn't afford to purchase your supplies, there were no freebies given by the state prison system.

There was a light-skinned West Indian named Isaac who was about twenty-eight years old. He kept pretty much to himself and no one knew what he was in for. We got somewhat friendly and I found out he was an avid reader with a pretty decent private library. My head had been changing toward the better, and after two years of not really using my mind, I had begun dealing in getting an education as well as a better understanding of myself and my life via reading. From Isaac I got Richard Wright's *Native Son*, Lillian Smith's *Strange Fruit*, and many other books that were relevant to my life.

All this reading and the discussions I had with Isaac and others got my mind to thinking. While reading John Oliver

Killen's *Youngblood*, a strong desire surged through my blood, a thirst to write, and write I did despite the fact that I didn't know where to put commas and quotation marks and I wasn't too sure about adverbs and pronouns. But that didn't stop me. I just let it all pour out. I almost literally vomited words on paper.

One day in my cell, I remember an incident that happened to me as a young boy in Babylon, Long Island, and wrote about it because it was related to my surging feeling toward writing.

At the beginning of World War II, my father hit the numbers and with his new airplane factory job, we moved to a house in the country way out on Long Island. I was enrolled in Babylon High School where the lack of blacks and Puerto Ricans was so apparent that the two or three of us there looked like little brown specks floating in a sea of milk.

I had a young English teacher who was so beautiful to me at age fifteen that I promptly fell in love with her, from afar. One day she asked the class to write a composition on anything we wished. I proceeded to write a two-and-a-half-page declaration of love. I wrote of my passion for her beauty, her wondrous hazel eyes, the softness of her curly chestnut-brown hair, the warmth of her well-stacked body. I included that I didn't particularly care for her adjectives, pronouns, verbs, and so forth, but could manage to live with them for her sake. All in all it was a composition of love and beauty.

I turned the composition in and carefully avoided meeting my English teacher's eyes, lest the burning love-light in mine betray me.

A few days later, we were called up to her desk one by one to retrieve our compositions. When my turn came, I went quickly to avoid her eyes. Looking from the comer of my eyes, I reached for my composition.

"Turn your paper over and read what's there." She smiled as she spoke.

I turned it over and there written in red pencil at the end was this note:

SON,
 Your punctuation is lousy, your grammar is nonexistent. Yet if you want to be a writer, you will be.
 P.S. We both love my wife.
                    [Signed],
                    Her Husband

All I could do was stare heartbroken at my English teacher, and her understanding smile almost made me blush through my brown skin.

I had by this time a little library of hand-picked books gotten from inmates who wanted to sell them or give them away because they were going home. I felt kind of like an intellectual and would sometimes have fantasies about having some of my own books alongside those of Killens, Wright, Smith, and others. Regardless, I had found something to do that was me. It was my safety valve. I had found how to express myself on paper and escape from the ugliness of that prison cell inside me.

My writings at first were recollections of free side—in the form of short stories and poems—and these progressed into writing my observations and feelings of the goings-on around me in a strange, brutal, ice-cold world called "prison." The system had tried to soften the harshness by labeling it "correctional institution" and by changing us from "prisoners" to "inmates." I often wondered if the officials' next step of fantasy would be to have this hell called "hotel" and us "guests." I wrote these thoughts down. I wrote about us humans in every aspect of our continual debasement, hiding my papers in fear of getting caught by the guards with such anti-prison-system writings.

We were subject at any time to a shakedown—a search of one's cell and person, usually without warning. Sometimes the guards would spring the shakedown in the wee hours of the morning, looking for contraband, weapons, and un-American writings, the last being anything that told the truth about what was happening inside the joint. Guards did not expect us to love the prison, but we had better not in any shape or form smear the integrity of the place, let alone the honor and fair-mindedness of its keepers. We, the kept, didn't have the right to be so ungrateful.

When I first started to set my mind to a routine of reading and learning, I had gotten some light kidding about it. I often wondered if it is just human nature to put down, even if in jest, the efforts of someone trying to do better. Many times the inmates would sit around and talk about past crimes, each trying to outdo the other with heroic details. There would be looks of admiration and words of praise, but when the conversation turned to bettering one's mind with books or discussions, there'd be some polite, "Yeah, yeah, that's great," and the attempt was buried under another round of negative bullshit.

I remember one day I had come from the prison library where an old white con librarian by the name of Joe had laid two heavy books on me, one was a dictionary and the other dealt with philosophy. I approached Pancho and Bayamon, who were leaning up against the prison wall.

Pancho, noticing the books under my arm, asked, "Hey, what's happening with them heavies under your arm?"

"I got them in the library. Joe the librarian recommended them to me. He said that this book on philosophy was a conglomeration of many schools of thought as to what the manifestation of life is all about."

"*Coño*," whistled Bayamon. "What he say?"

"Yeah," said Pancho, looking a little hurt that a couple of words like *conglomeration* and *manifestation* could send him up a dead end. "What the hell does that mean?"

Oh boy. That's when I went into my grandstanding. I cleared my throat and feeling like some doctor of letters or something, hung it out for my two illiterate *hermanos*.

"*Conglomeration* means many things put together and *manifestation* is what comes out of it. Diggit!"

Pancho nodded and looked very wise. Bayamon only said, "Man, that's some heavy shit."

"Anyway, I got these books from the old man to broaden my intellect. Man, I'm tired of reading westerns, murder mysteries, and bullshit short heists."

"*Tu qué?* I didn't know your intellect needed broadening." Bayamon moved around me and I just watched him inspect my backside.

"Whatta you think, Pancho? His intellect is pretty broad now. Don't you think?"

I just stood there patiently, waiting for him to get his cracks in so I could continue what to me was serious conversation.

"Maybe it can stand to be a little broader." Pancho helped Bayamon out. "You know the saying, 'The broader, the badder.'"

"It's pronounced *better*, not *badder*."

"You see, Pancho. Piri's intellect is getting broader all the time."

I waited for them to stop laughing. I laughed only to be a good sport, and finally got going again.

"Be serious, you guys. Like I said, one book is on philosophy and the other's a dictionary to broad—to enlarge my vocabulary."

"Wow, *amigo*." Pancho was on a teasing streak. I almost knew what was coming. "Ain't your vocabulary enlarged enough? *Caramba*, you beat it often enough."

"Wow, ain't *nada* sacred. *Coño*, if I jack off, that's my business."

"Well, keep your shades down. The reflection shows in the window across from your cell."

"You know something, *pendejo*," I smiled friendly-like. You're a manifestation of a conglomeration of a real genuine twenty-two-carat *maricón*."

Pancho went into some mincing girlish step, said in a high voice, "Oh, please, tell me more," and swished his behind from side to side, ending with, "I do so want to broaden my intellect."

Bayamon and Pancho roared with laughter. I had to burst out laughing, too.

"O.K., O.K., see you around, lowbrows." I started to walk away.

"Hey, *panita*. Don't go away mad. I was only kidding."

"I ain't mad. It's just that there is a lot to be learned in books, man, and like I'm into some heavy stuff."

"Heavy is right," roared Pancho. "Them two fucking words must have weighed at least a couple hundred pounds apiece."

I waved a disgusted but friendly see-ya-around, checked out across the cellblock, and found myself trying to quote something I had read. What I remembered was: "Many times in history great minds have been ridiculed by others because of their faithful quest for knowledge."

After that barrage of ribbing, it made me feel a little better to join the ranks of history's greats who suffered the slings and arrows but never copped a plea.

One time a group of us were sitting in the yard, yakking. Conversations made time go, but most of them were about how to rip somebody off. You could, if you wanted to, cop yourself a doctorate in the arts of hijacking, swindling, burglary, assault, or murder. One had to be choosy about picking academic peers who were interested in creative writing, art, and music and who also had good ideas for going into some legitimate business.

Bayamon was saying, "Yeah, like getting a franchise on a take-out-a-fried-chicken stand."

L'il Henry put a downer on the franchise idea. "You can't get a franchise on a chicken coop, let alone a chicken business, if you're an ex-con."

"So," Bayamon came back, "you get one of your relatives who ain't got a record to be the dummy head."

Pancho grinned and cracked, "Fat chance for that. L'il Henry was the one without a record and he screwed that up."

L'il Henry laughed good-naturedly and contented himself with an up-yours gesture as answer.

"All bullshit aside," continued Bayamon, "it's a snap. The relative is the front and you're the real biggie behind the scenes. And you make money hand over fist. Everybody likes fried chicken."

Pancho looked thoughtfully at Bayamon and asked, "Er, and how much does this franchise run to?"

Bayamon scratched his knee and screwed his face up doing numbers inside his head. "Uh, about ten, twenty thousand bucks."

Politely, I asked, "Hey, *hermano*. Will you tell me something? Where's the money coming from to buy the franchise?"

"Yeah," broke in Pancho. "Like, say the five of us wanted to go into business, and, like, we all save our money in here. And since we're all pulling five years or more, at ten cents a day, five of us is fifty cents a day, that's...$182.50 a year. So if we each pull, let's say, three years more, we'd have all together $547.50."

"Yeah," I said. "Still kinda short, huh?"

We all laughed. Zorro, who had been quiet up to now, said, "Say, I got a good idea." His eyes gleamed mischievously.

"Yeah," Bayamon said guardedly.

"We all meet on the outside, see, and we plan a big job together, pull it, and then go legit. We'd all be partners in a take-a-chicken-home with a big neon sign in the shape of a chicken without no feathers." He stopped.

Bayamon glared at him. "We were talking about being legit from the get-set-go."

Zorro shrugged his shoulders and innocently said, "Oh, say, Pancho, count up how many years we'd need for, say, $10,000."

"Oh, shit," said Zorro.

Bayamon took the ribbing but added, "I meant from the jump, when we get out, to get the bread between us legitimately."

I interrupted, "Hey, you forgot something."

"Yeah?"

"Yeah. We'd all be back in here one more time. Like, remember, it's parole violation for ex-convicts to hang around together."

We laughed. We all knew we had just been bullshitting to pass the time. But I couldn't help wondering how we could ever help not meeting each other often, since we all came from the same area in El Barrio.

Another inmate was sitting nearby and his conversation had been rolling by my ears along with others within hearing distance. I looked his way. It was a swarthy-complexioned con named Mack. "Yeah," he was saying, "when I get me out of here, I'm gonna get me a stash of schmack and turn on..." He seemed to go into some kind of ecstasy just talking about that damn poison. I turned him off. Too much negative prison conversation centered on drugs. As an ex-junkie, I had already gotten the drug shit out of my mind as well as out of my system.

"Hey, bro. Wanna make a fourth for whist?"

"Sure, Bayamon, *por qué no?*"

"You be my partner, O.K.?"

"Sure, Bayamon, *por qué no?*" I picked up my hand, but my thoughts kept hanging on: Man, I ain't never gonna let cockroaches eat up my mind with drugs again. Diggit!

"I bid three no trump," I said.

"I'll take that for four—down the river—no trump." Zorro grinned maliciously.

"GOD REST YE MERRY, GENTLEMEN"

A lot of men in prison don't pay attention to the holidays like Christmas, New Year's, and Thanksgiving. I did. Each and every little holiday I paid attention to and thought about what it commemorated.

Christmas-time behind bars loaded the prison atmosphere with a pollen of sheer melancholia. Months before Christmas, inmate artists were busy painting portraits of other inmates or of loved ones from photos, as well as landscapes and abstracts. The wood-carvers were turning out intricately designed jewel boxes, statuettes, and serving trays with painted scenes and with words like "To Mother" or "To My Wife" brought into relief with tinfoil painfully peeled from the wrapping in cigarette packs. Beautiful leather work was turned out. Materials were gotten by hook or by crook, and any kind of available tool was used. Wood was given a fine finish with a piece of broken glass used as a plane and tooth powder as a fine abrasive. Stain, varnish, and shellac were somehow procured, shellac being the hardest to get because too many inmates liked to strain it through a loaf of prison bread, mix it with fruit juice, and proceed to get stoned.

All this activity was for Christmas presents to loved ones on free side. Financially, those of us with talent for making things had it made. The works of art were sold to less talented inmates for cartons of tailor-mades, which could be traded for fresh milk, eggs, steak, homemade cakes, custom-made prison clothes, or used for gambling. It made you affluent enough to be able to get the nicer things in prison society.

Christmas was just fifteen shopping days away. I had finished work in the paint gang, had my supper of "pasta-fazool," soup and coffee, and had gone back to my cell to wait for recreation time. The trumpet blew, giving the signal. I stood at the bars of my cell.

"Hey, *panín*. You ain't going to the rec hall?"

"Uh-uh." I shook my head no. "I got some sewing to do."

Bayamon smiled. "I dig, *amigo*," and moved on.

I found a needle and thread and got busy with a piece of strong cord about three feet long and a pair of heavy woolen socks.

By the time recreation period was over and the cons were making it back to their cells, I had finished. I dug with pride my tailoring abilities. I had a sling I could put around my neck, and at each end of the cord was a sock, sewed so that it resembled a miniature seaman's bag. I placed a pint-size jar in each sock, pulled the top tight, placed the cord around my neck, put on my bulky winter prison jacket, and felt that the jars on either side fit snugly against my ribs. You couldn't even tell they were there. Pancho passed by.

"You finished your shit yet?" he whispered.

"Like *chévere*, Pancho." I smiled and, pulling my jacket open, watched for some kind of admiration from him at my handiwork.

Pancho just said, "Looks O.K....We all start tomorrow morning, right? That's the word. They'll be having the stuff."

"Right," I said, giving him a shitty look. Maybe I should have embroidered the damn socks.

Next morning we were lined up in the main cellblock as usual, each cellblock then being marched at thirty-second intervals to the great mess hall. The ten of us blockmates kept looking at one another and winking while waiting our turn to march, each with his sling of socks and jars hidden under his overcoat. Gordo was nervous, and in Spanish whispered that we had better cut the smiles and winks before any of the hacks got suspicious. We all grew dead serious as we shook our heads in agreement.

As we marched into the mess hall, I was confident our plan couldn't fail. We had worked it out too carefully. Wearing our overcoats wouldn't arouse any suspicion because right after mess hall we were supposed to cut out into the yard and head for our jobs in the paint shop. All we had to do was take care of business while the hacks weren't looking.

We marched into the mess hall, picked up our trays, copped the breakfast offered, and—it hit us that something had gone wrong. I could see Zorro's lips silently sounding, "What the hell happened?"

Jesus, I thought. *All this planning and it's a bust.* We all sat down, and our gang, which consisted of about thirty men, ate breakfast noisily with the exception of ten who were so down at the mouth our tongues could have been used for shoehorns.

Breakfast over, we filed out into the cold and crunched our way across the snow-filled yard to the paint shop.

Down in the shop, it took special maneuvering to sneak the slings off, take the jars out of the socks, and arrange them innocently in our lockers. When we had changed into our work clothes and were waiting for our assignments, we got ourselves close together, joking and laughing while we tried to get our heads straight on the next move.

"Christ Almighty. They always serve prunes and apricots on Tuesday for breakfast. Why'd they switch? Ya think they're wise to us?"

"Aw, hell, nothing like that," I said. "Just probably ran out of the shit."

Pancho shook his head sadly. "We can't make that Christmas cheer without that stuff. Je-suss, we got everything to make it—yeast...sugar...empty quart mayonnaise jars—all we need is the apricots and prunes to make fine wine or better."

"Yeah," Gordo said sadly. "The longer it fermented, the better it would have been. Maybe the warden's wise. Maybe we better get rid of the evidence."

"Cool yourself," said L'il Henry. "Let's try again

tomorrow.

"I don't think I can stand the strain," said Gordo. It's like planning a breakout."

"Come on, Gordo. It won't be *coquito*, but it will beat a blank."

Bayamon leaned over to me confidentially and whispered, "Square business, *panín*. You think we're being set up?"

"Naw, we'd have been busted in the mess hall, socks, jars, and all. We'll check with Russo in the kitchen and get the what's-what on tomorrow's breakfast menu."

Jesus, the whole shit's nerve-wracking. We sent a message to Russo and the word was "Go." Apricots and prunes for sure, tomorrow A.M.

Next morning it was all we could do to keep a straight face. We had pulled the impossible. With our ten portions of apricots and prunes, plus twenty other contributions, we were on our way. We pulled it off right under the hacks' noses.

I saw Russo, a trusty in the mess hall, approaching us with a bag. As usual, he was smoking a "ginnie stinker."

"Hey, Russo, thanks for the tip. It was right on the ball," whispered Gordo.

"So why didn't ya tell me from the beginning? I was figuring at first you guys were constipated."

We laughed. "Naw, nothing like that, Russo," Johnny Lee said.

"Anyway, I got a proposition for you guys. I ain't got the time or the inclination to take the trouble to make the stuff. However, if youse guys give me a quart jar of homemade booze, I will donate free of charge..." and Russo opened his swag bag and pulled out two quart cans of prunes and apricots. We checked to see if any hacks were close by. The coast was clear.

"It's a deal. Man, with this much, we got strong stuff brewing."

"See ya around, fellers. Don't forget, a quart or better of the juice. Oh, yeah, I forgot. Here's a can opener. Give it back. They count everything in the kitchen."

The following days were spent with a most beautiful sense of anticipation. The time went smoother because we ten comrades had something to look forward to—homemade wine or maybe something stronger. Every time one of us had a chance, we'd check the jars to see how the fermentation was coming along. We had stacked them carefully near the huge asbestos-covered steam pipes that ran the length of the wall in the back of the paint shop. The heat speeded up the chemical change.

It was no secret that all over the prison different cliques were getting their own thing together like us. Others, not wanting to go through the trouble or to take a chance on being busted and having to spend the holidays in the box (solitary confinement), would rather buy the juice from different wine merchants.

Besides homemade juice, you could always make a connection for barbiturates, all kinds of colored pills, wild pot grown by trustees working outside the wall, and shellac that may have been strained but was sudden death when you least expected it. For the elite inmates with money working for them inside and free side, there could be real Scotch or whatever via hack connections. There were hacks who made a hundred bucks on a fifth of tailor-made booze. But if you had the wealth, you didn't mind spending it.

For a week before Christmas, there was a tree in the chapel, one in the main hall of the cellblocks, and one in the mess hall, all brightly and gaily decorated by trusty cons with light bulbs, tin, tinsel, and other trimmings donated by outside groups. "Silent Night, Holy Night" was everywhere you went. Christmas carols were picked out on guitars or played blues style on trumpets, and Spanish carols from childhood were sung. You could check into your cell at any hour during the day, put on your earphones, and "God Rest Ye Merry, Gentlemen" would blow your mind.

We strove to enjoy Christmas with some semblance of normality. Very few of us ever let on we were bugged. Give in to depression and the next step was hanging yourself or taking a high dive off the top tier into a pool of rippling cement forty or fifty feet below.

Even before Christmas Day, inmates were exchanging presents with members of their clique, and it was nothing to see trustees, playing postman or Santa Claus, make the round of cellblocks, delivering presents and bringing some back.

If wrapping paper was hard to come by, gifts were carefully wrapped in toilet paper and were accepted graciously. The gifts ranged from a carton of cigarettes to a couple of loose smokes, to a special sandwich made up of groceries from home. Whatever it was, you gave what you had and accepted appreciatively what you got. It was a *chévere* feeling to sit quietly in your cell and open up toilet-paper-wrapped Christmas gifts with "Merry Xmas" written on them.

Among the gifts I got one Christmas were an O'Henry candy bar, some smokes, a Danish-ham sandwich, and a ring carved out of a red die—the last was from Bayamon. I hoped he liked the one I made for him out of a peach pit. A package came from Johnny Lee. I could hear several recipients of his gifts yelling out to him, "Hey, Johnny Lee, you're too much," or, "Got to admit it, buddy boy, ain't never got a present like this before." I opened Johnny's gift. It was a booklet with hand-printed words and hand-drawn pictures, a ten-page pornographic booklet entitled "The Rise and Fall of the Warden's Daughter." I made up my mind not to get caught with this one, else I'd really be up the creek.

Pancho and I sat in the paint shop playing heads-up poker. From the latest inspection of our wine cellar, it was clear that it would be only a short time before we'd all be enjoying the fruits of our labor. Johnny Lee walked up, sat down, and was dealt a hand without his asking. We automatically bet without talking bets.

"Thank you for your dirty-book present," Pancho said.

"Aw, it ain't nothing." Johnny Lee looked pleased. "Hey," he added as an afterthought, "every book I gave out is different, so you guys are perfectly free to swap around."

Pancho beamed. "You finished yours yet, Piri?"

I nodded yes.

"I'll trade you. Mine's name is——"

"Hark, the Herald Angel Got Copped," broke in Johnny Lee with a laugh. "Shit, fellers, it ain't that I'm sick or something. It's just that people are so uptight about sex. I'm just humorous about it, especially after coming from a long line of Amish brethren or something. Shit, my parents were so uptight about sex, I think I got conceived by my old man giving my mother a kiss on the forehead."

We all laughed till the tears ran down into our socks when all of a sudden there was a loud explosion like some pipe or gas had exploded. Everybody jumped up like his *culo* was on fire. The blast had come from the direction of our wine supply.

Billy the hack walked slowly toward the blast. He unlocked the wire door. I was almost tempted to invite him to use the entrance we had cut through the wire at the far corner. We heard him fumbling around in the semi-darkness and there were ten sets of fingers crossed that our Christmas cheer would not be discovered. But like wishful thinking...

Billy came back out and with a faint smile calmly asked, "Would anybody like to claim this goddamn shit?"

Nobody claimed it. Billy the hack went back into the semi-darkness and proceeded to smash the jars one by one with blows from his club. Then he came out and said, "Hey, one of you men, grab a trash can and clean up them broken jars."

Pancho beat me to the jump. Ten minutes or so later, he came back and sat at the table. His face was serious as hell, then began to spread into a beautiful sunrise of a smile, and his softly whispered words proved there was still a God in Heaven.

"Billy the hack missed a jar. I got it in my swag bag!"

And like, man, it was something to see. Ten sunrise smiles lighting up the gloom.

IS THERE NO WAY OUT?

L'il Henry and I were walking up and down the length of the prison yard, chewing the rag about this and that, when suddenly the prison siren split the air with its wail. The sound rose and fell again and again like some unearthly thing in the throes of ear-shattering pain. We stopped walking and looked at each other. All around us, inmates and guards were doing the same.

"It's a break, brother," L'il Henry ventured a guess.

"What makes you think so?" I asked, though I believed he was dead right.

"The way that siren's blasting, it can only be two things—breakout, or we're about to be bombed."

I nodded my head in agreement.

Breakout it was. The hacks were rigid and their heads swung from side to side.

"How the hell did he or they ever get outside the walls?" Henry asked the chilly air. "This damn place is maximum security."

"Maybe he got help from the outside," I answered.

"Well, he better have a fast car waiting, a nearby airport with a private plane, plenty of money, and a passport to some place where extradition is a dirty word."

The trumpet blew. Lockup time had been pushed ahead because someone had taken a thousand-to-one shot and maybe made it. There was no doubt the majority of us were rooting for whoever it was to make it; if this escape from the slams was a success, there was hope for someone else making it. All you needed was to stop being afraid of dying by shucking off the care of living and go for broke. The word came passing through from mouth to mouth. Some con named Red had split.

The guards moved the line at a fast clip and we were herded into our cells. Keys were turned and master locks thrown with an urgency that had an odor of fear mixed with hate. The suspense in the air was shared by hacks and cons alike.

"You think he got away?" a loud voice from way out in A-Block asked. And a voice from my own C-Block yelled back, "I sure fuckin' hope so, man. It's about time one of us got a break."

"Shut your goddamn mouth up there," broke in another voice.

"Who the fuck are you?" came back a reply.

"I'm a guard, goddamnit. Now shut up."

"Well, la-de-da, motherfucker. You can kiss my ass."

"Tough guy, eh? I'd like to know where your voice is coming from. Come on. Be a man and let me know."

"From 110th Street, motherfucker."

There was some laughter from us cons, not mirthful, but to let our fellow con know we were with him. A voice with a kidding sound to it yelled out to the angry con, "Hey, you meant that about the hack kissing your ass?"

"Damn right I meant it."

"Well, er, I'd be careful about that shit. There's a lotta cats in here might like to take you up on that."

More laughter...drowned out by the blasting escape siren.

"Hey, people, cool it. Hack's on his way up there," a con's voice warned.

Everyone cooled it and the hack found nothing but innocence in every cell. No sooner had his footsteps faded away than our voices became alive again. Some source of information via con blared out, "Hey, Red made the break from outside. The cat worked on the farm!"

I laid on the bed and refused to stare out through the green-painted bars of my cell, contenting myself with checking out the steel ceiling of a damn hole in the wall called C-5-13.

I mused over all the times I had thought about escape. There isn't a convict who doesn't think about it sometimes— or all the time. I was no exception. I used to spend hours in my cell dreaming up ways to break out. I strained my memory to recall books I had read with prison breaks in them, as well as films I'd seen, most of which ended with the escapees being riddled by machine-gun fire and falling like flies from the rope they were climbing to get over the wall. Sometimes they'd make it to a fast get-away car and roar off to a short-lived freedom that ended in a gun battle with the police or some small-town sheriff. The only one I could think of who came close to escaping was Paul Muni in *I Am a Fugitive from a Chain Gang*, and he was last seen being hunted and melting into the shadowy fog-filled night after saying goodbye to his sweetheart as he mumbled something about, "They've made an animal out of me."

There weren't many success stories about escapes. The legendary Willie Sutton ranked as one of the best escape artists in prisondom and even he was eventually recaptured. The last time he got busted, they handed him what I believe totaled 155 years.

I thought of escaping by hiding under the prison trucks that brought in supplies. I thought of dyeing my prison grays a dark green and brown for summer escape and snow white for a winter walk-away...of braiding me a rope out of odds and ends and trying for an anchor shot over the wall. I thought of cutting into one of the huge ventilators that led up to the roof—I'd lower myself down four or five stories to the ground, leap over or dig under a fifteen-foot electrified wire fence, slip invisibly by guards with automatic weapons, and having no outside get-away car waiting for me, nonchalantly hitch me a ride to El Barrio, Nueva York, El Big Apple. *After all, my brown skin shouldn't keep me from getting a ride from some good folks*—whose relatives were probably guards in the prison.

Man, I even thought of learning yoga and copping some kind of mystical power whereby I could slow my heart down to nothing, play dead, and get my corpse shipped home C.O.D., whereupon I would bring myself back to life, free as a bird, even if it meant scaring the living crap out of whoever opened the coffin. Silly fantasies, eh? But I wasn't the only one thinking about freedom.

There was Flaco, who was always a little weird in his moodiness and uptight attitudes. While most of us thought about escape, he talked about it constantly despite our warnings to cool it lest he be busted head-first into solitary accompanied by some painful injuries played on his head. I ran into him in the prison yard one day and he motioned me over to a spot at the side of the wall not occupied by cons or hacks.

"Hey man, I think I finally hit on how to get the fuck outta here." Flaco tried to talk out of the side of his mouth like a good self-respecting con is supposed to, but his declaration came out as loud and clear as if he were running for some kind of office.

"*Coño*, man, cool it. I don't mind so much getting busted for really escaping, but to get a jive-ass bust for just talking about it—no way."

Flaco shrugged his shoulders, looked at me tolerantly, and, apparently deciding to overlook my nervousness or coolness, went on.

"Ya see this deck of cards?"

I nodded. "You're getting out by doing card tricks?"

"Na, stupid. This is scientific."

"Yeah?" I was getting worried about Flaco.

"Yeah." He went on as if patience was difficult to muster.

"Look. I read in a book that there was this prisoner in a dungeon and he was rotting away with guards beating on him from time to time and rats doing the same."

"So?" I smiled, trying to look interested.

"So, he gets a hold of an ordinary deck of playing cards, some matches, and a small piece of lead pipe with a screw cap on each end."

"Yeah, and...?"

Flaco was really warming up. "And he takes only the

cards with the red numbers on them and cuts out the red-painted pieces of all the cards."

"Where'd he get the knife in solitary, let alone matches, playing cards, not to mention a lead pipe with two screw caps on each end?"

"Turkey," Flaco good-humoredly insulted me. "The motherfucker had good connections."

I nodded and said, "That sounds logical, not to mention fair. Go on."

"Well, he takes all the red pieces of the playing cards and wets them into a soggy mass, then caps one end of the pipe and jams the soggy red mass into the open end, stamping them in good and tight. He fills up the empty space with plain pieces of the deck and closes up the pipe tight. He puts one end of the pipe into his mouth and with the matches sets fire to a piece of wool..."

I looked at Flaco and he added, "...that he ripped from his cell stool. Then he begins to heat the pipe."

"So how does that get him out?" I pushed.

"Simple, man. The heat at the one end of the pipe causes some kind of gas buildup from the chemical in the red pieces of playing cards, causing a vacuum. The pressure got so great inside that the pipe did a wan-go—bombs away. It blew up."

"Asshole," I said disgustedly. "How did that help him get away?"

"By blowing his head off. He wanted to commit suicide."

"You believe the crap about the playing cards?"

"Sure do. I'm getting the stuff all together and—"

"You gonna blow your head off?" I asked gently.

"Naw, brother, just the lock at the front gate."

"Oh, I see. Good luck," and I walked away from him, the prison's one and only Puerto Rican anarchist.

Sometime later I ran into Flaco again and out of curiosity asked how he was making out with his bomb. He shook his head sadly and said he had everything but the piece of pipe that had to be specially made with grooves and caps on each end.

"Wish you luck, Flaco." I grinned, then added, "Too bad

you don't have the connections that cat had who blew off his head."

"I'll get it yet. Don't worry. It works, I tell you, powerful bomb. There wasn't enough left of that guy in the book to put on a spoon. The cell walls were just dripping with him after the explosion. Shit, with that kind of power, I could bring the whole fuckin' wall down."

Flaco walked away, leaving me thinking about the walls of Jericho. I laughed out loud. Humor is a great safety valve. I stared after Flaco's skinny five-foot-five frame ambling off, walking street-wise hip. Funny how his dark-brown eyes were always shining bright. They seemed to give color to his otherwise pale skin. Caramba, *Flaco should watch his cool. He's looking for a flip trip to a nut factory.* But I wondered if it was really possible to make a bomb out of a deck of cards.

My mind turned to Red, who was a *blanco*. The word on the grapevine was that he may have made it safely outside the prison walls.

He had worked outside the walls on the prison farm, where he drove a tractor. From somewhere out there, he had lifted some civilian clothes, but instead of cutting out, he had come back to the prison, hung his gray convict uniform on the huge steel back gates of the prison, and attached a note damning the whole system. The delay was a bad loss of precious time. His prison clothes and note had been found, and the hunt was on. What he did could only have been an act of defiance and contempt for the prison system.

Red was captured, and, according to cons and some guards, he had offered no resistance, but surrendered quietly. That didn't stop the hell that fell on him. He was brought back to the prison and beaten to a pulp, with practically all his teeth smashed out of his mouth. Some said they could not recognize Red after that beating. They smashed him so much his red blood covered his white color. I swore to myself one more time that I was going to survive.

I stepped out into the bright sunshine of the prison yard

but didn't enjoy its Sunday warmth. It seemed somehow dulled by the ever-present color of blue hack uniforms and the drab gray of prisoner clothes. I leaned against a railing and caught a blurred reflection of myself in a dirty window. I felt my face with an indifferent hand. There was no doubt about it. It wasn't the same Piri who had come into prison over what seemed a thousand years ago. The reflection that stared back at me was young-old, harder, and prison-wise. My days in prison had passed slowly through a hole in time and had become three years.

I stared harder at the dirt-streaked glass and it seemed I could see a montage of past events of my life in this concentration camp of inhuman debasement. I saw the past. I knew the present and was vaguely trying to see if the dirty windowpane would project a future when I was brought back from my reverie by the sound of familiar voices.

Bayamon, Zorro, L'il Henry, and Juan de Jesus were engaged in animated conversation. I studied Juan, who was very well-educated and who spoke seldom and only to the point. Juan was holding a prison-worn copy of the *New York Times*. L'il Henry saw me, and as always with anyone he considered a friend, his dark face broke out in a grin and he waved for me to come over. I waved and thought how there wasn't a real evil bone in L'il Henry's body. His was a real honest free spirit who acted without malice, but somehow it always seemed to get him in trouble. The hacks who had no love for any skin that wasn't white seemed determined to wipe out the good-natured feeling in L'il Henry's heart, but to no avail.

I walked slowly toward the group, waving a greeting. "*Hola, hermanos.*"

"Hey, brother Piri, come and join us," said Juan. His face was grim though under control. The headlines in our two-week old New York Times read: ASSASSINATION OF TRUMAN FOILED IN GUNFIGHT OUTSIDE BLAIR HOUSE; PUERTO RICAN PLOTTER, GUARD DIE.

I let out a soft whistle. The attack had occurred on November 2, 1950. I had known about the Nationalist Party's struggle for independence for Puerto Rico ever since I was a youngster. It always stood for political change through peaceful and legal channels. U*n antipático* broke into my thoughts.

"Cripes, ain't that the stupidest thing in the world to pull. Imagine trying to kill off the President of the United States. Crazy people, man, gotta be crazy people. Only a fucking fanatic would do a thing like that. Shit, what does Puerto Rico need independence for? Christ sakes, it's got the United States on its side. It don't have a damn thing to worry about. Who's gonna mess with Puerto Rico with such a big gun on its side?"

"Nobody except the people who want to be free," answered Juan. "And to correct you further, the big gun is not on our side. It is pointed at our heads."

"Well, shit, man, if the United States is so damn bad, what the hell are so many Puerto Ricans doing living in the States? That's downright ungrateful," the unfriendly inmate pushed.

"I am for a *Puerto Rico libre*," Juan continued. "I'm an ingrate. Speaking for myself and for freedom-loving Puerto Ricans, I can say we have nothing to be grateful for. We've been bought by the simple expediency of making us so economically dependent on the United States for our existence that the majority of us are afraid to go it alone as a free country and are content to lean on the security of the United States as one would lean on a crutch."

I turned and walked away, barely hearing the response of the antagonized inmate. In my own way, I had to work off the crushing oppressiveness of the prison atmosphere. It was pretty hard hearing about freedom for a country when you yourself were not personally free. Political awareness was not too big a thing with me at that time. Survival was.

NOTHING LIKE THE REAL THING

L ove is where you find it, but in prison, most times, it's in your head and hand. The natural sex drive becomes almost unbearable as months grow into years, and the absence of a woman to love becomes the greatest sense of lonely pain next to the agonized yearning for freedom. If one didn't make an attempt to control the sexual drive, it could become an all-out obsession. Inmates resorted to all kinds of substitutes. At movies in the prison auditorium, for instance, they'd rub their penises through their pants while checking out the women in a film and reach a release. This was the cool way of doing it. Others weren't so cool and would masturbate one another or themselves openly. It was dark in the movies, but there were also a lot of guards. Some saw what was happening and ignored it or were amused. Other guards busted the inmates for enjoying a short heist.

One inmate came up with the idea—not, I suppose, original with him—to fill a medium-sized long jar with oleomargarine and insert it an angle in a slit he cut in his mattress. When the lights went out and the hack made his rounds, this inventive human being would turn on his stomach and take care of business.

There were many other ways; masturbation was first but homosexuals or prison-made "joy-boys" came in second. This way was risky, but it went on nevertheless. Joy-boys were less respected than true homosexuals and were used by jailhouse gorillas who by right of might, threats or treats, would commit sodomy with their victims as well as force them to perform fellatio. To compound this, the gorillas would also put the joy-boys out to hustle their favors on other inmates in exchange for jailhouse goodies, which had to be brought back to daddy. Outside in the streets, they would simply be called "pimps."

I dealt in fantasies. Like maybe taking trips to other planets and imagining the beautiful women on Venus, since the Goddess of Love was supposed to live there. Many times I'd lie there, close my eyes, and say to myself, *Well, where to tonight? Oh, maybe to Huntspoint Palace or Manhattan Center. I'll catch Tito Puente and his orchestra. I'll dance my ass off tonight. Or maybe a walk in Central Park.* I'd go through my mental address book of the world's most beautiful *mujeres* and settle on a girl, and we'd go for a walk in the park, have dinner at Sardi's, and dance till early morning.

Sexual fantasies were developed into a fine art by the delicate process of retouching photographs of women in newspapers and magazines. *Life* was a great source of material for beautiful photographs of models and actresses in various poses, scantily clothed or in bikini bathing suits. Resourceful inmates would make the figure naked by the simple process of bleaching out the parts of the body that were clothed. They used nothing more than water, a soft cloth, and light circular rubbing motions, turning to a clean part of the cloth every time the preceding part was covered with printer's ink. Eventually, after some important touch-ups here and there with colored pencils, a most saleable pinup was created. Some of them could have been centerfold pieces in any top girlie magazine. Many of these retouched photographs with their recreated nipples and pubic hairs were bound into prison-made short-heist books, complete with stories that when read under prison conditions—meaning lack of women—would literally make an inmate's sexual hairs stand on end. These booklets, whether rented or sold, brought in a good price in terms of cigarettes.

I tried to produce some until a close buddy got busted

with a stash of short-heist material in his cell. He had to go through a whole lot of hassle to prove he wasn't a sexual deviate, but just a nice, clean, young inmate who recognized the need of inmates for sexual release in the form of fantasies and was only helping alleviate the pressures of abstinence while trying to make a buck.

I quit cold. I didn't want to chance being sent to the "Siberia of America," Dannemora. They had a hospital for the insane. There was no way to tell the prison system that we men inside the walls were not sexually maladjusted, but only sexually deprived. If all the magazine photographs of beautiful women I retouched were known to the guards, I stood a good chance of having something like "potential sex maniac" stamped on my prison record, thereby slimming my already slim chances of making parole. But I wasn't alone. They could have busted the whole prison population, guards included since they were among the best customers for short-heist books. The only exceptions were a few religious converts. The homosexuals were doing the same thing as us except their retouched pinups were photographs of men, and some of them got so carried away with the touch-up jobs that even King Kong would have been envious at the size of the added manhood in the photographs.

I almost hated to give up the artwork because it was profitable. But it was too dangerous, and if caught, the erroneous charge of sickie was on the record for keeps. Not for me. I wasn't going to get busted for reckless fantasizing.

There's no way to describe fully the indignities and debasement suffered by the joy-boys. Intimidated by threats of death or mutilation, these youngsters lacked the strength and courage to resist and thus became human receptacles for other inmates' sexual release. The victims had no recourse. If they complained to the guards, they would condemn themselves to the lowest wrung on the prison ladder—the rat, informer, squealer, *chota*—all these meaning the same, and if they had to endure the contempt of the guards and inmates alike for having succumbed to being girl-boys, being squealers was even worse. No wonder the highest rate of mental illness was among these youngsters, not to mention suicide attempts, successful and unsuccessful.

Too many young inmates accepted another inmate's help of fist power against his enemies only to find he eventually had to fight off his erstwhile benefactor because the payment demanded for the assistance was sexual. Physical protection was equated with supplying sexual gratification to your protector. Face trouble alone and, win or lose, at least you didn't have to pay off in Shakespeare's literal pound of flesh.

The basic training in survival that I had received on my ghetto streets stood me in good stead in this Christian hellhole. I used to chant constantly to myself the lesson I learned in the Tombs: *I came in here my father's son...I'll be damned if I go out my mother's daughter.* As Bayamon had said, I learned to grow eyes in the back of my head and force every pore of my body to become an ear. One could be knocked unconscious in some secluded part of the prison and be raped by one or many, unobserved by guards who might just ignore what was happening. It didn't matter whose fault it was. Conscious or not, the traumatic experience was ineradicable.

In some of our conversations, we would talk about women's prisons and wonder if they were as bad as ours. We didn't always agree on which was worse, but we surely agreed wholeheartedly that if society wouldn't permit us the normality of conjugal visits or weekend passes home, then it should at least make men's and women's prisons co-ed. Society was treating us both as subhuman. By being able to treat each other as peers, man to woman, and to fall in love with each other, we could retrieve our identity as human beings. It would ease the pain of loneliness and fulfill the human right to feel love and express emotions.

Hell! Our bodies had been placed in prison, physically incarcerated, but how in heaven can society incarcerate human emotions? All the substitutes for normal relationships in prison do not make the inmates perverted. It is society that is perverted by perpetuating this negation of normal expressions of love.

Many of the killings in prison were sex-related. I remember the grapevine buzzing with the news of one such incident. There was a jailhouse gorilla named Pug who had hit sexually on a young inmate called Angelo and had him so terrorized he told no one, not even his brother, Dominick, who was serving time in the same prison, something rare. Dominick, who worked in the mess hall, began to notice Angelo's nervous condition, the bags under his eyes from sleepless nights, and his jumpiness if anyone came on him too suddenly. His brother asked him time and again what the hell was wrong with him, but Angelo wouldn't say until, according to the grapevine, he was raped again by Pug and some of his friends. Angelo poured out his shame to his brother, and Dominick immediately asked him to set up a clandestine meeting with Pug. Pug picked a secluded place behind the outdoor showers in the main yard, a spot shielded from the guards in the yard and those on the wall.

Angelo met with Pug and suddenly Dominick was there too, armed with two kitchen knives used to slice meat. He tossed one to his kid brother and they proceeded to puncture Pug to the extent of thirty or more holes. Pug died without falling down, propped against the prison wall. The brothers walked away smoothly. Nobody seemed to have witnessed what had gone down.

But they were busted by the guards. An inmate had seen them, informed, turned state's evidence, and got his freedom with a stepped-up parole. And the brothers, again according to the everloving grapevine, got fifteen-to thirty-year sentences tacked on to their original convictions, to be served consecutively.

I myself never carried a guilt complex for sexual fantasizing. The choice was that or a state of limbo via insanity. It kept many of us from blowing up. Like was said in prison, "You can't die from lack of sex, but you sure as hell can shrivel up." Diggit!

I sat in the front row of the baseball stand with a pad and pencil in my hand, trying to get some writing done.

"Hey, Piri, wanna play shortstop?" It was L'il Henry. I

stared down at him and shook my head no.

"How about pitching?"

My head still shook no.

"Wanna umpire home plate?"

"I don't want to play, Henry. I got some writing to do."

"You're writing a book or something?"

"I'm writing whatever I see, hear, and feel about what's happening in this damn place. I've found me in what I can do best, and it's in my writing."

I waited for L'il Henry's reply to hear if he was going to wisecrack at my wanting to be a recorder of all this hell around us. I should have known better because L'il Henry's voice reflected some kind of pride in me.

"Brother, your kind of talent is most needed, 'cause a human can shout off some soapbox in the middle of the prison yard and it reaches just so far. But putting all this inhumanity into writings, you can reach out to the whole world."

I grinned from ear to ear, glad to hear his words since letting yourself be known in prison as a poet or writer often exposed you to ridicule from inmates who still couldn't see tomorrow because of yesterday.

"I'm sure glad as hell to hear you feel this way. Here, take a look."

I watched L'il Henry quietly read the things I had felt were important enough to jot down. Finally, he stopped reading, but didn't say anything for a long while. My voice sounded somewhat insecure as I asked, "Hey, brother, it isn't bad, is it? I mean taking into consideration the mistakes in spelling and grammar. It ain't all that bad?"

"Far from it, Brother Piri." L'il Henry's voice glowed. "It's beautiful. You got a gift for recording. I'm reading and I'm seeing pictures in your words. You got a real talent. Use it well."

"I intend to, L'il Henry."

L'il Henry smiled and waved a see-you-later. I watched him walk away, pounding his fist into a worn baseball glove.

My eyes continued to roam around the prison yard. There

were hundreds upon hundreds of inmates involved in all kinds of activities, from kid convicts to white-haired old-timers, all sizes and shapes, different nationalities, different heritages. The only things in common were the gray uniforms, the numbers in place of names, and the pulling of time. My ears picked up metal clanging against metal and I turned to watch some inmates playing horseshoes. I heard side bets being made on the possibility of the next throw being a ringer. Again my eyes roamed and they took in the inmates who sat at green metal tables playing the usual games. Some games were for fun and there was laughter, while others were being played in dead earnest for cigarettes. There were few arguments at these games. It would have been crazy to cheat at a table where at least one inmate was doing time for murder or some kind of rip-up assault.

My eyes roamed some more and I dug the guards placed around the yard at vantage points. I looked up at the towers on the wall; the guards stationed there had clear vision to every part of the prison yard, except for a few blind spots known to con and guard alike. Most looked bored, but it did-n't stop them from keeping a watchful eye on us residents.

I checked out a group of inmates who hung out together and had a rumor going for them of being rats, *chotas*, finks, and squealers. They always seemed tense and jumpy and would stay close to wherever the guards were, frightened of the other inmates. I shook my head thinking that informers had a hard way to go in a prison, hated by the cons and only tolerated by the guards. Probably they were still in one piece because it was only a rumor, but once it was established as truth, they were lucky if the warden shipped them to another prison before they suddenly became "accident prone."

I heard the sounds of *salsa* coming from the east wall and my eyes took in some Puerto Ricans and blacks working out Afro-Latin music on congas, bongos, timbales, guitars, and the ever-present cow bells. My mind threw me back to the outside where I saw myself with a *chévere* woman doing some together *alma* steps in a dance hall. I followed the beat by making clicking sounds.

I caught a group of brother inmates sitting in a semi-circle and knew they were into the religion of Islam. I had sat with them many times. To my way of thinking, the Muslims were not aloof from the rest of the prison population in an arrogant manner. It was just the way they carried themselves that made them seem aloof. They walked in dignity and their conversations were not the usual negative prison bull sessions. They were interested in the rights of nonwhites in a white world. They were serious about their religion and put forth their thoughts, carefully based on their beliefs, in quiet, soft-spoken voices, with courtesy and self-respect.

Their presence in the prison could not help rubbing off on us nonwhites. No more than it could help rubbing the prison officials the wrong way. The system did not quite know how to deal with inmates who looked them straight in the eye and whose faces showed calmness and a lack of fear. The prison system wanted to see looks of humility and servility, even looks of anger, rage, and hate. These could be analyzed. But blacks and browns who walked tall as peers was something to fear.

In all my time in prison, I never saw a Muslim cop a plea, even while being brutally beaten. Their walking tall had, without a doubt, rubbed off on me and penetrated deep into my heart.

My ears caught some conversation in another direction. "I swear to God I'm gonna kill her when I get out."

"What's burning you up, Mack?"

"I just got a visit yesterday. My brother told me my wife is shacking up with the goddamn janitor of our building. Ain't that a bitch?"

"Holy hell, Mack. You've been in eight years already. You gotta expect her to have feelings. I mean, she's human, too. You'd be fucking around now, too, wouldn't you? Face it. It's a reality."

"Man, that ain't what's burning me up. I'm a guy who's respected on the Lower East Side. Everybody looks up to me on Fourth Street, and she brings me down by opening her goddamn legs to a plain ordinary janitor. If she hadda do it,

did she hafta do it with the guy that throws out our garbage?
Aw, shee-it."

I thought about my girl Trina and blew away the mental
picture of her and a damn janitor. I turned to eavesdrop on
two young blacks who were talking in a low, tense tone.

"What you burning about, Slim?"

"That goddamn racist hack been on my back again."

"Called you 'nigger' again?"

"Nay, man. Last time he called me that shit, I told him
where the fuck to go."

"Yeah, I remember—caused you some good time besides
gettin' your head whipped in the box."

"I ain't forgetting that. Anyway, he don't call me 'nigger'
no more. He just calls me 'boy.'"

"Better than 'nigger,' ain't it?"

"Man, he calls me 'boy' and does it in a tone of voice like
he was calling his own son. He's a slick motherfucker if he
thinks smearing his insult with Vaseline is gonna make it
easier for me to take."

"Do you know what that S.O.B. calls his nightstick?"

"Yep, 'nigger stick,' but most of them do."

"I'd sure be pleasured to ram that stick up his nose."

"Day is coming, Brother Al. Day is coming..."

Their conversation died away as I began to roll a Bull
Durham. I made it with one hand and felt pleased I'd become
an expert in the art of rolling your own. I lit up and inhaled
deeply. My eyes hit on a couple of homosexuals making their
way to where I was sitting. Some good-natured remarks were
being thrown their way. They just smiled and sat below me.
The breeze brought a scent of perfume my way. I closed my
eyes and thought of women and opened them again and saw
homosexuals. These weren't prison-made. They had come into
prison as homosexuals and were proud of being so. One with
red hair was named Margie. The story is that she, and that's
what everyone better call her, wasted her old man on free
side for running away with another woman, a real natural
woman, that is. Ellie, the other, and I don't know how true
the story is, was in for attempted rape. The story is that Ellie

tried hard as hell to prove she was a man by trying to rape a young girl who was living with a lesbian. Nothing happened, but the lesbian got uptight and had Ellie busted. Ellie and Margie didn't go the rough way of those forced into sex acts. In this jailhouse, they, and others like them, were for those who were interested at a premium.

To some cons, they were the closest women moving, next to a natural woman. And it's *mucho* hard after being locked up for a long time not to start looking at them with almost the same kind of feelings that a man would put out toward a woman. I remembered one time...

A young effeminate inmate was assigned to the paint gang. His arrival sparked the usual looks and remarks.

"Hey, look at that pretty..."

"What's your name, honey?"

I had looked up from the paintbrushes I was cleaning and saw the newcomer smiling coquettishly at one and all. As the days passed, I found myself looking more and more at the young inmate, whose name was Alec. Somehow we got into a conversation in a corner of the paint shop.

"What's your name?" Alec asked me.

"Piri." I smiled, and from the corner of my eye I could see the other cons smiling knowingly. I ignored them.

"You in long?" Alec asked.

"Long enough." I didn't like to be reminded.

"I'm in for five years."

"That so?" I answered.

Alec nodded and looked at me for a long time, and like his eyes were saying it all. Then he said it.

"I like you a whole lot. You don't come on wrong and strong like the others. You're polite. I'd like to be your old lady."

I looked at him and couldn't help smelling the perfumed lotion he was wearing. It cut through the smell of paint and turpentine like a flower garden. I looked around to see if the others were still digging us. Nobody was. I felt myself getting warm as hell inside, and for a while I couldn't think of anything except having sex. My mind surged with memories of sex on the outside. I was reliving my lovemaking with a woman, and this young inmate who was so willing was making it unbearable for me.

Alec smiled again and said, "There's nothing wrong in our getting together. It's good for you 'cause you can have love from me, and it's good for me 'cause I can have the same. Besides, I'd be left alone by the others once you and me get together."

I just looked at Alec. I felt beads of sweat just under my skin. I had the most fantastic urge to hold that human in my arms and make believe it was a woman. I looked again. Alec was like a woman, his mannerisms and the softness of voice, and his build was slender. He walked kind of graceful-like. I glanced around, but no one was looking.

"What do you say, Piri? There's nothing wrong with us making it together." I felt my hand reach out and my fingers caress Alec's face, his hair. I began to feel my nostrils dilating, and, goddamn to hell, my breath was starting to come out in short heavy gasps. Alec came closer to me and I put my arms around him. He tilted his head back and his lips started to purse. *My God, we're going to kiss.* My emotions roared at me. I let go of Alec and sprang back as if I had just touched a red-hot oven. I stood there shaking my head from side to side.

"What's wrong, Piri?" Alec whispered, glancing around to see if we had been observed.

"Nothing, man, nothing. It's not you. It's me. I can't cut this. Sorry, Alec. See you around, O.K.?"

I left Alec looking at me with wide-open innocent eyes. I moved over to some guys playing checkers. My head was reeling 'cause I knew once I got into a bag like that I could start digging all the Alecs of the world.

I hadn't been putting Alec down for his way of living, but I couldn't put down my way of living either. For me there couldn't be any substitute for a woman. I had peeked over at Alec and he was still staring my way in lonely silence.

The trumpet blew and I walked off the grandstand. *Man,*

a whole lot of men have pulled time without digging another man's behind, and I'd better get my mind on something else beside nooky-nooky. The real thing wasn't nowhere to be found inside those goddamn walls.

CONVICTS FIRST AND PATIENTS SECOND

I lay in one of the white-painted beds that were spaced evenly all around the room. It was the first time I had been in the hospital ward in Great Meadows Correctional Institution, and I wondered if I had been wise in asking for the operation. There was so much scuttlebutt about the inadequate medical treatment—inmates were treated as prisoners first and patients second. But I needed the operation.

Every time my nature rose, it was binding and painful. The only way out of the discomfort was circumcision. An inmate nurse came in and gave me something to kill the pain of the operation.

"We'll give it time to take effect and then in you go. Your dong will be a foot shorter when you come out." The inmate nurse laughed.

I looked at him, a tall, thin white man of about thirty-five years of age. I didn't smile at his joke but just said, "Just take the foreskin off. I need the rest of it."

"I'm with you, buddy. I feel the same about my Oscar."

I watched him go about his business of bedpans and laid-out inmates. My eyes dug the different patients. Some were very old, white-haired inmates, maybe just trying to die in gentle dignity. Some of the younger ones had on bandages that no doubt covered wounds, either from a fight with another inmate or from some fury at the end of a guard's night stick.

One had his forearm and wrists bandaged. It might have

been from anything, but probably a suicide attempt. I listened to soft, pain-filled groans and uneven snoring and heard the coughing of tired old lungs too wasted even to stand fresh air. A voice lost between sleep and wakefulness was reliving a scene long ago at home and talking love with someone named Clara.

"Hey, you're on, buddy. Can you walk to the operating room, or are you too high on Demerols?"

"I can walk." I didn't feel any effects at all. I eased out of bed, stone-cold sober, and holding onto the back of my flapping hospital gown, I followed the inmate nurse. My eyes caught some large bottles on a shelf and I winced, 'cause one of them contained somebody's enlarged heart—pickled. The name on it was Chang, or something like that. It had belonged to a former Chinese inmate. Another looked like a liver.

Christ, I thought, *I hope to hell this operation's a success. I don't want my personals floating around in some damn jar with some kind of label like, "Oops, we cut too much."*

We went into a small operating room and I recognized the prison doctor. Man, did we cons have little faith in him. Whenever we went up to sick call, he had a cure for anything. His favorite was a pill called "brown bomber," guaranteed to make you hemorrhage on a toilet bowl moving your bowels. Another was a red liquid that was supposed to calm everything. "Saltpeter" was its name. How many times he'd stand there as if listening to your health problem and before you finished or even began he had already written his favorite prescription.

One time I told him, "I got a pain right here, Doctor"—pointing to my chest—"near the old bullet wound."

"So have I," he answered professionally. "Take two of these and get some rest."

I couldn't help thinking about the other doctor. Being a dentist was his bag. Oh, man, don't ever get a bad tooth in prison. Don't even be locked up in your cell with an abscess. At times the throbbing pain is so bad you want to smash your head into the cell bars. All kinds of advice are available from sympathetic *amigo* cons, like shoving tobacco into the hole in your tooth, or slushing cold water around it, or plugging up the hole with an aspirin if you have one or using mind over matter to will the pain away. And, like, better believe it, there was no such thing as saving a tooth by having it filled. Somehow, to our prison dentist, every bad tooth was beyond redemption, like it was easier for him to pull it than fill it. There were a lot of young cats looking like old men with gummy grins because so many teeth had been pulled unnecessarily.

I had gone on to thinking about the fingers I had broken at different times trying to catch line drives and how they had been set crookedly, when I heard the doctor's voice.

"It should be a tough fight." He gestured for me to lie on the operating table. For the first time I noticed a radio was playing. It was a heavyweight championship fight, Jersey Joe Walcott fighting Rocky Marciano.

The doctor slipped on some rubber gloves and pinched the head of my penis. "Feel this?" he asked.

"Yes, I can."

"Uhmmm, I think Marciano can take Walcott," he said to the inmate nurse.

"Sure will, Doctor, Walcott's over the hill." I looked up at the ceiling and from the corner of my eyes saw a scalpel in the doctor's hand. He pulled my foreskin and cut. My whole body arched. "Hey, Jesus Christ Almighty, Doctor, whatever was given to me ain't taken effect. I can feel it."

"Relax, this won't take too long." His ears were tuned to some lefts and rights being slashed into Jersey Joe's face and midsection. "There, that's a nice combination," he said, again to the inmate nurse.

My body was as taut as if rigor mortis had set in. I saw him take a needle and catgut and begin to put in stitches, which I later found out was called "putting on the collar." As the needle went in, pain-sweat gushed into my eyes.

"Goddammit," I grunted out. "I can feel every fuckin' bit of it."

"It's all in your mind, feller. Now stop squirming and stop

your damn whining, I'm almost through."

He paused in the middle of a stitch. Walcott caught Marciano with a jawbreaking right. The doctor went back to stitching as Marciano recovered and dropped Jersey Joe with a devastating right.

"There, we're finished, take him back."

The inmate nurse eased me off onto a stretcher and wheeled me back to the ward.

"Some fight, eh?" He was making conversation.

"Shit, yeah." I gritted my teeth. "I'm glad as hell I won."

"Uh? Oh, yeah," he laughed. "Well, you still got most of it left. You know, sometimes the pain is all in your mind," he parroted the doctor's words.

"Hey, man," I muttered as I slid gingerly from the stretcher to the bed, "believe me, I know when pain is in my mind and when it's in my body. That shit didn't take effect."

"What can I tell you, that's the way the cookie crumbles." And he damn near ran back to finish listening to the slaughter on the radio.

I lay there, not moving, trying to forget the pain, and all of a sudden I didn't feel any pain. The medication had finally worked and I drifted off to sleep.

Oh, holy mackerel, gee whiz, diggit!!!

I'm home. I can't believe it. I'm really back. Oh, man, is Trina gonna be surprised. Christ, that *muchacha* is too much, waiting for me all these years.

As I cut down Lexington Avenue, headed for 104th Street, I could see Trina in my heart. Curly black hair, large dark eyes, and skin like soft cream. She was tiny, about five-foot-two, with beautiful white teeth that set off the most *chévere* pug nose ever and a *cuerpo* that was made to order in one of God's special molds. All this *belleza* weighed no more than a hundred and five pounds of warm, loving delight.

Oh, Trina, I ain't ever gonna fuck up again. No more jailhouses, no place, no time. You and me...we're gonna check out of El Barrio and find some place in Puerto Rico and raise lambs and make mucho babies. We gonna find us a place that ain't got gray streets and dusty, curling chimney smoke. We ain't gonna live in a ghetto that's old a thousand years back. There ain't gonna be no more despair and anger for us. Shit, baby, we'll get us a finca way up in the mountains of Borinquen with all kinds of mango trees, *aguacates*, and all the other goodie trees. We'll make mucho beautiful love by the light of multi-colored sunsets and wake up to the sunrise with more of the same. Baby, *chica*, like, no more I'm un numero called "18193." I'm Piri like always, and I'm free. Caramba, hon-ee, splitting to Puerto Rico will mean we can cover ourselves with blankets of warm Puerto Rican breeze and dig all kinds of music from singing *pajaritos* and chirping *coquís*.

I ran up the stairs, not even pausing as my old street *amigos* shouted greetings, "Welcome back, Piri." "Hey, man, glad to see you..."

I banged on the door and Trina opened up. She was wearing a gossamer nightgown, like I knew she would.

Her face got a look of shook-up.

"Surprise!"

She stood there, paralyzed.

"Yeah, it's me, baby. It's me, Piri. I'm out, I'm back, honey."

Trina's face puckered up, her lips began to tremble, and tears flowed down her cheeks like two tiny waterfalls.

She jumped into my arms and I kicked the door shut, holding her tight as life. We kissed each other over and over again, as Adam and Eve must have kissed in awareness of their *chévere* love.

"You've been gone so long, Piri."

She felt good in my arms. "Ain't never splitting again, *corazón*, never," I rocked her gently in my embrace. "Jesus, I've missed you. I needed you, I've wanted you."

We just stood there looking at each other. Her feelings for me were the same.

"We've wasted so much time between us, baby." Trina nodded and putting a tiny finger to her mouth, warned me to be quiet. She listened in the direction of the rooms where the rest of her family lay sleeping. Reassured no one was stirring, she took my hand and quietly led me to her room.

She closed the bedroom door gently and came into my arms. She held me tight. I dug her by the light of the red blinking sign from the store across the way. Neither of us said a word. She moved away and got into bed. I undressed with the sound of silent speed and eased my way next to the warmness that she was, and we held each other gently and made first love like children long lost from each other. Her gasp of pain was given gladly. I made love to her, trying to be as gentle as a saint, and loving as a man.

It was good. It was beauty...it was us. We felt each other explode into a rainbow of release and floated entwined through paradise.

"Oh, baby," I exhaled the words softly. "You don't know how much I missed you, how much I wanted you."

"It was the same for me, my love." Trina caressed my face. We both smelled of love. I felt myself falling asleep.

She came closer into my arms. My hand stroked her soft breasts. I listened to her even breathing and felt her heart beat beneath my fingertips. I let myself fall asleep to the timing of her heart.

I hadn't been asleep too long when I was shaken and a harsh voice shouted something at me. I fought to wake up. Who the hell had broken into the room? Through sleep-struck eyes, I saw a guard.

"Hey," I yelled. "What the hell do you want?"

"This ain't no damn hotel. Breakfast time is now or never," he growled.

I sat up in bed and rubbed my eyes. *Aw, shit!* I was back in prison. *Just a dream. Christ, it was so real.*

I split to breakfast and stared at the lumpy oatmeal before me. *Aw, shit!*

Man, like in prison, fantasies can make you blow your mind.

Madness on My Shoulder

Inmates can be locked up for the night in a reasonably good frame of mind and can come out in the morning like wounded wolves. One morning, I stood at my cell door waiting to get out. The main lock was pulled open, and I stepped out on the tier, took a first look through the giant barred windows, and shivered at the sight of the swirling snow outside.

I sure as hell hate wintertime in prison, I thought, *but then l hate all the seasons inside this joint. Yeah, but maybe wintertime a little more 'cause there's not enough heat to keep the cellblocks warm.*

I made my way down the tier and met Pancho coming out of his cell. I gave him a comradely slap on the back and started to say, "Hey, *hermano*, how you doing?" But I never got to finish. Pancho grabbed a fistful of the front of my shirt and smashed me against the cell bars, lifting me until I was hanging there tiptoed. His voice was a low-pitched snarl.

"Don't you put your fucking hands on me. I'll break your goddamn jaw."

Pancho's free hand was clenched tight around something metal that gleamed sharply. He held the blade down by his knee, ready to put all the crushing power of his weight behind it.

"You fuck with me again and Ill bust your throat wide open."

I dug Pancho's eyes and saw that they didn't know me at all. They had the kind of cold shining brightness that spelled out he was stone-bugged. I knew the signs. I'd been that route many times before, so full of frustration and locked-up anger that it didn't matter who it was. The first person to even smile at you was going to bear the full brunt of a sickness called "stir-crazy." It's like a fever, and for some it comes and goes. For others it never goes and that means game-time for a good mind that snapped.

The inmates walking by just kept on walking. Some said, "Hey, Pancho, easy man," but didn't stop. They were as sympathetic as could be toward my predicament, but it wasn't their business, only Pancho's and mine. There were two things I could do, being so damned off balance. I could use my knee and bash in his groin, or try to talk him down. Pancho was one of my prison *amigos*. He hadn't hit me yet. I made the split-second decision—I'd try to talk him down from his jailhouse madness.

I lifted both my hands, palms out, in a gesture of non-violence.

"Pancho." I said his name soft and friendly. "What's the matter, *hermano*? Be cool. If I've done anything for you to have sweats with me, I'm sorry, man. Really, I am."

Pancho raised me a little higher on my toes, keeping me pinned against the bars. His face was frozen in contorted rage. I kept my voice in the same soft and friendly tone.

"Pancho, diggit, it's me, Piri. *Coño*, man, ease off. Think, man. Just catch on to yourself and think."

I peeked at Pancho's right hand at the side of his knee. It was trembling like it was gonna be sprung any second into my face. I could damn near feel my bloody gullet protruding from a slit throat. I braced myself and found the little added balance I needed for leverage to ram my knee between his legs.

"Pancho. *Por Dios, panín*, take it smooth. *Es Piri*, man. I'm sorry if I bugged you." I held my breath. Nothing in me wanted to hurt Pancho. I made my face smile low-keyed. "Easy, *panín*, easy."

I watched and Pancho's face finally began to unfreeze. From a mask of stone, it began to warm into a human being once again. His hold on me relaxed, though our eyes remained fixed on each other's. I felt the heels of my shoes touch flat bottom again. I didn't have to feel my forehead to know it was covered with sweat.

Pancho's breathing started to slow down and become normal. We just stood there, staring at each other. The moment I was free of his grasp, anger rose in me, mixed with embarrassment from the undignified way he had hung me up in front of the other inmates. I felt my fists begin to close, but fought down the impulse to revenge myself with the understanding that Pancho had not been Pancho for that short piece of time.

Pancho looked at me and shook his head in bewilderment. His face clearly said, "What the hell was I going to do?" He shrugged his shoulders, mumbled an inarticulate apology, and moved away from me quickly. I watched his retreating back, pushed my shirt into my pants, took a deep breath, and followed after. I joined the line down on the flats and met the eyes of the cons who had seen what had gone down. Some shook their heads; one motioned toward Pancho and tapped the side of his own head. I heard Bayamon whisper behind me, "*Coño*, Pancho almost flipped his brains."

I said nothing. The line began to move into the mess hall. I thought, *Yeah, Pancho almost flipped his brains and I almost got caught in the middle of it. Got to be careful with Pancho from now on. Christ, I wonder what the hell could've bugged him so. Maybe bad news from home.*

And another part of my mind replied *Something that's bugging us all—this nuthouse that goes under the name "correctional institution." Rehabilitation. Bullshit. This goddamn place can only rehabilitate you into a mouth-foaming maniac, if you let it.*

Don't let it, Piri, my mind advised me.

I won't, diggit, my *corazón* answered back.

We sat in the mess hall eating breakfast and someone's eyes were on me. It was Pancho, sitting across from me. I stared back at him and watched his face break into a half-smile. He whispered, "Hey, Piri." I nodded and gulped on a mouthful of Comstock coffee.

"Uh, say, you want my prunes and apricots?" I broke out in a grin. Pancho was trying his best to say he was damn sorry.

"*Chevere*," I whispered. "Good looking out."

Pancho pushed the dish over to me and winked. I winked back. I didn't really want the prunes, but how could I turn down his sincere peace offering?

"Thanks, *hermano*."

"*De nada*, bro."

I ate his prunes and apricots and listened to the defensive part of my mind playing over and over like a broken record, *Better watch Pancho from now on, 'cause maybe next time...Better watch Pancho from now on, 'cause maybe next time...*

Pancho smiled at me and I smiled back.

Once every so often, an activity that was wholly made up of inmates would come our way. I called it "Jailhouse Show Time." It provided for a sense of involvement. The program included music, songs, dancing, and comedy, and each ethnic group was represented: country music by the whites, rhythm and blues by the blacks, and Latin music by the Spanish-speaking inmates. It went over big because music has the magic of bringing everybody together in common enjoyment, if only for a short while.

The best of one such show was a skit about rehabilitation. The two cons involved had somehow gotten permission from the warden to use a guard's jacket, cap, and nightstick. I guess the warden gave the O.K., figuring it might better relations between cons and hacks.

In the skit, the inmate in guard's getup proceeded to play musical bumps on his partner. Every time he'd bash him on the head, he'd say, "You all rehabilitated yet?" And when he'd received the answer, "Ah think so, *sir*," he'd deliver another whack to the con along with the words, "What? Listen, you damn con, you gotta be sure if you're gonna get your ass outta here"—and *whacko*, he'd lay another make-believe lump on his partner's head. Every time the con got whacked, his legs would do a wobbly number until finally he fell to his knees. Another whack and he was down on his hands. Another, and he fell flat on his face.

"Is you rehabilitated yet?" came the question. The inmate on the floor rolled over on his back, weakly raised himself on one elbow, and said, "Sure am, boss. Ah's almost dead." He got one last wrack for his troubles then pulled out a paper lily, crossed his arms over his chest, and played dead. Meanwhile, the uniformed inmate looked out at the audience with a pleased expression on his face and said, "And these cons got the damn nerve saying there ain't no rehabilitation going on in here."

The skit brought a lot of grim laughs from us inmates, but there was a cold, uncomfortable silence of stares from the guards, with the exception of a few who dug the graveyard humor and looked embarrassed. I caught a glimpse of the warden's face. It was noncommittal, but his constant scratching at the side of his nose led me to believe that noway and nohow would permission ever be given again to have the honor and dignity of a guard's uniform so despicably besmirched. The skit got a great hand from us, and the line "Is you rehabilitated yet?" floated through the prison for many a day.

One thing about show time inside the place—it gave a great opportunity for all the *chévere* prisoners' talents to shine through. At the end of it all, we, the audience, gave the performers a standing ovation, regardless of race or color. There would be time enough the following day to return to a division of skin hues.

PRISON IS DEATH ON LIVING TISSUE

It's very human to cry, but tears do nothing for one's image in prison. Yet every prisoner sheds tears at one time or another, sometimes crying quietly in his lonely cell, biting his forefinger in helplessness, and hoping no one hears his sounds of sorrow. Some find temporary relief in weeping—others just go off the deep end...

One night the agonized screams bounced off the steel and concrete of the cellblock, making the echoes reverberate in multiplications of themselves. I literally rose half a foot off my mattress, the sleep blowing away from my eyes. *Goddammit—what next? Who the hell is getting wasted this time?*

"Hang up! Hang up!" came con voices intermingled with the screams.

"Hack on the tier—hack on the tier—this stupid motherfucker cut his wrist again."

I rubbed the back of my neck wearily and checked out my Timex wrist watch. Two-thirty A.M.

"Why don't that sonofabitch do the job on himself quietly and die without making so much fucking noise? It's tough enough sleeping in this birdcage without his bullshit screaming."

I recognized the voice. It was L'il Henry. I heard guards running, their feet making thunder-like sounds on the metal tier floors.

"What's happening, Henry?" I called out.

"It's that same bastard, Piri—you know, Cholly. He's always cutting his wrists."

"Yeah, I know who it is. Looks like he don't cut good enough—he's never died yet."

"It's a game with him, man. A sick game. He always waits for when it's nearly time for the hack to make his rounds and then goes into this bullshit."

The screams had now turned into low, pitiful moaning and groaning.

"Christ, don't be too hard on the cat, L'il Henry. He just can't pull the time—it's pulled him."

"Bullshit. He don't wanna die no more than I do. He's just sick in the head, man. He pulls that bullshit to get attention, that's all. He ain't never cut nowhere near the big veins. That stupid asshole just slashes himself nicely and politely to make blood run and then throws himself on the floor with his arm flung out the bars and screams like it's game-time. He just wants attention."

"Hey, you big mouths up there, can that talking unless you want a keep-lock on your asses."

No con can give you a keep-lock, so it had to be a guard.

"Fuck you," said L'il Henry, and kept quiet.

Qué mierda!, *Cholly gotta be crazy*. Yet my mind could understand what he felt. Maybe he didn't have anyone on the outside who cared for him, and certainly no one on the inside.

"Hey, L'il Henry," I called out in a low voice.

"Yeah, brother?"

"You think maybe he cut himself right this time?"

"Naw. If he meant to go all the way he wouldn't have made such a fuss. When you gonna kill yourself for real, you don't broadcast. You do it nice and quiet and as privately as possible. But you can bet he's gonna be on his way to some prison nuthouse." L'il Henry chuckled without sounding mean.

"Prison nuthouse? What the hell do you think we're in now?" I whispered grimly.

"Not everybody in here is nuts, little brother. But where he's probably going, everybody is stone crazy from the guards on down."

L'il Henry yawned sleepily and added, "If he ain't crazy

now, he'll surely go all the way once he's sent there."

"Knock it off, you guys," a sleepy voice politely requested. We knocked it off.

What a way to go, I thought to myself. *What a damn way to go.*

The work on the new classrooms was coming along. I stopped counting how many cement blocks I had laid to make partitions, paid no attention to the tons of lime, sand, and cement I had mixed, and hardly noticed my calloused hands and aching back. I worked hard because I knew it would make the long days pass faster. I was getting short again. I'd be seeing the Parole Board one more time, and nobody, but nobody, inside the walls can shut Parole Board time out of his mind completely. It's a fact that when a con starts getting short, somehow trouble seems to pick up on him. Sometimes from hacks getting heavy on him, but most times from cons who know he's seeing the board soon.

I had just finished lining up a row of cement blocks with a plumb bob, checking to make sure it was straight. All around me were other cons, some working and bullshitting, others just bullshitting. I had just laid some cement blocks and was tapping them into place with my trowel when I heard someone making squeaky sounds from between compressed lips. A sound that was a universal expression in prison, it meant getting hit on. I went on working, vaguely wondering who was getting the jailhouse flowers. The sound kept on coming. I looked up. The hack was about forty feet away, engrossed in conversation. The sound had stopped. I picked up my line and adjusted it at both ends to make ready to lay another row of blocks, then heard the squeaky shithouse sounds again. But this time, from the corner of my eye, I caught sight of a convict who was neither black nor white— a mulatto. He wasn't too long in the prison, but from his looks, he had been to plenty of others.

I ignored him. I had no proof it was me he was sounding on, and if I drew on him with angry words he could always say it wasn't me. I lost myself in my troweling. The sound came again, this time *mucho* close. Like from two feet away. I looked up and there was nobody between him and me. The cat had a smile on his face. I just looked at him. He was heavyset, about five feet eleven inches. His skin was something like white, but his features were totally like black. His kinky hair was bright red. We stared at each other. I spoke softly.

"O.K., man, you had your kicks, so like enough. There's nothing happening with me. I'm straight. Now that you know where I'm at, be cool. No hard feelings, all right?"

I stared at him with an ice-cold expression.

"What's your name, feller? Mine's Sweet."

Oh, wow, he's heavy sweat for a cat named "Sweet."

I nodded and dug my eyes into his.

"It's 18193, man—just 18193."

I turned to go back to work and he got the squeaks again.

My voice came out harder this time, but still suppressing out-and-out anger. "Look, man. Don't be a turkey, O.K.? I already told you there's nothing happening here. Why don't you take your ideas to some other corner? You might be lucky and hit."

I turned away, trembling inside with molten lava that was threatening to erupt. I saw my level on the ground and bent over to pick it up. I straightened up abruptly. That red-kinky-haired sick sonofabitch had goosed me right between the shoulder blades of my ass—and now there was no more room for words. He must have had some kind of victory assured in his mind, 'cause he didn't even jump back when I swung the long, heavy wooden level like a baseball bat. I caught him square on his left elbow and before the surprise of pain made space on his face, I smashed the level into his ribs. He doubled over to one side and I caught him on the shoulder bone. That knocked him down on one knee and he put his left arm out, shaking his hand to signal that I shouldn't waste him anymore.

God knows I wanted to kill him. Like all the past shits of being in prison could be eased off by my taking it all out on him. But somewhere in my mind something kept telling me that if I killed him, a lot of time was going to be handed me on top of what I already had. If I kept pounding him with my level, sooner or later I was gonna catch him right and kill him.

My foot, encased in its prison boot, swung from way back and caught him on the side of his mouth. He fell back against the newly laid concrete blocks. His eyes were glassy, but they could still see. One hand was trying to ward off anything else that might come his way, the other was trying to help him get up. His voice came out scared and damned hoarse.

"Time, man—time! Didn't mean to fuck with you, didn't mean no shit at all. I was just trying to see where you were at so I could beat you out of some of your groceries. Can't blame a guy for trying to gorilla extra smokes and grit."

I let him get up and watched him trying to scrape his face clean of the wet cement that had come from my clodhopper. I found myself talking like a stone killer. "Next time there ain't gonna be no next time for you, motherfucker. Now *please* get out of my face."

He put both hands palm out in a gesture of comprehension and moved away. I watched him go and put him down in my mind as someone else not to turn my back on—ever. Next time it might be a knife and not a goose. I looked around. The hack was still lost in conversation. The cons who had been digging what had gone down went back to work and bullshitting. I went back to laying cement blocks.

"Aw, shit," I said out loud. "That sonofabitch fell up against my wall and threw it dead out of level."

"Going again, eh?" Bayamon fell into step with me on the line of cons.

"Yeah, you too?"

"Why not? I mean it's for something good, ain't it?"

"Damn right." I smiled. "It helps save lives, don't it."

Bayamon grinned good-naturedly. We were marched—I managed as usual to walk—to the main cell hall.

"How many times have you gone already, Piri?" Bayamon whispered, checking out the hack at the same time. I held up from talking 'cause the guard was looking our way and I didn't feel like risking a keep-lock for something as dumb as whispering on line. The guard's eyes went somewhere else and I answered.

"Enough times to cop me a gold pin."

"Shit, man," Bayamon replied, "you only get that when you go over a gallon."

I smiled, trying to keep vanity out of my face.

"Let's go," said the guard. We marched into the designated area and my eyes took in a table that had doughnuts and cold bottles of Coca-Cola. Red Cross nurses were busily drawing blood from inmates' arms. Others were passing around the doughnuts and Coke.

A friendly atmosphere was created between the nurses and the cons, but the many guards lining the corridor were doing all kinds of numbers with eyes that were all over the place to make sure no inmate got out of line. *Christ,* I thought, *what do they expect us to do—jump the nurses and rape them?*

A middle-aged nurse motioned to me, but from past experience I knew I had to wait till the guard gave me the O.K.

"This way, please," she said. The guard nodded his head and I followed her to a cot and lay down. All around me, other men were likewise stretched out. The nurse smiled at me and rubbed my arm with alcohol, then slipped a rubber cord around my biceps and brought out a fine-looking vein. She pushed a needle into it and said, "You've been here before."

"Sure have. Enough for a gold button." I stopped talking because my eye had caught a hack looking dead at me with a face that plainly said, "No fraternizing." This didn't stop the nurse from talking.

"You men are really doing a fine thing in donating your blood."

Jesus, lady, I said to myself. *Every day this damn place is taking it away from us one way or the other. It's almost a damn pleasure to be able to give it of our own free will.* I just smiled.

A young nurse asked an inmate who had finished, "Are you feeling all right?" She helped him up. His face was a little pale, and she must have held him a bit too close, because two hacks quickly lifted him away from her and let him lie down on a side cot. *Man, what a drag!*

"Well, that was fast." I looked up at the middle-aged nurse and nodded. She helped me off the cot.

"Would you like some doughnuts and Coca-Cola?" asked a young nurse. I nodded yes and, sitting to one side, I munched slowly and let the cold soda run down my throat, like hoping its iciness might wash away the unnatural fever this goddamn prison had infected me with.

"You finished?" I didn't look in the hack's direction. I swallowed some more Coke, leaving a little in the bottle, then nodded yes at him with an impassive wooden face and gently set the almost empty bottle down on the table.

"You can finish it if you want," the hack said, not unkindly.

"I've had enough," I responded in the same coin. "Besides, Coca-Cola don't mean that much to me."

"What does?" he asked, and his eyes were full of suspicious *mierda*.

I thought of telling him, *The opportunity to hear the sound of women's voices and the help it gives in reminding me that I wasn't born in this prison, even though it seems as if I've been in one all my fucking life.*

Instead, I looked at him, scratched my nose, and answered, "The doughnuts. I got a real thing for them."

The hack smiled and said, "Oh, I see," and reaching over to the table, copped a couple more doughnuts and placed them in my hands.

"Here you are, feller. Enjoy them. Well, what do you say?"

"Thank you very much." The fever inside me was a little cooler.

"O.K., feller, get on your line." He pointed.

I gently held the doughnuts all the way back to my cell. We were locked in. I sat on the edge of the bed and stared at them fuckin' doughnuts until I horseshoed them one at a time into the open-mouth toilet bowl and with the point of my shoe flushed them double zeroes out of my life.

Is You
Rehabilitated Yet?

I sat in the yard feeling down in the dumps. I played around with a dandelion, deciding whether or not to pluck it from its rightful place in the earth, just because I had the power to do so. I had just seen the Parole Board, on August 27, 1953, and had been given two more years. My case was stamped: RECONSIDERATION ONLY. *Two more years before they'll even reconsider my appeal.*

On the day my case was heard, forty to sixty other prisoners had gone before the board and each had been given the space of six minutes in which to determine if he was "rehabilitated" and ready to be turned loose in society. We nonwhites could not help seeing the most unfair ratio of releases for whites. We could not help feeling that not being white made us seem the more dangerous and therefore subject to "Not now, maybe the next time around you'll be released." Didn't they know there was no such thing as rehabilitation inside the walls?

Anger choked my throat as I relived my appearance before the board. I went by them so fast it seemed I had gone through a greased revolving door. *Two goddamn more years! Damn their hearts!* For a long while after, I had made a point of not looking any con or hack in the face because of the bitterness and rage in my eyes. They might have taken it personally and violence could have broken loose.

It had taken me almost ten weeks to fight down the bitterness and get my head together to write a letter of recon-

sideration to the board, dated November 10, 1953. I had torn
up a lot of angry pages before I finally settled on a letter I
could send them. I had written the letter, not exactly as I
wanted to, but as I felt it had to be if I was going to escape
being buried alive on top of the ground for the full extent of
my fifteen-year sentence.

I looked at my fingers caressing the dandelion and saw
the cracked rawness of a million tons of brick masonry. I'd
joined the construction gang to build school classrooms with
cement-block partitions and cement stuccoing, and little by
little had become a damn good brickmason—but not good
enough to be an instructor, not because of a lack of skill but
because of a lack of white-skin pigmentation.

Although I had been recommended for the position by a
former white con instructor who had changed jobs, the prison
system gave it to a white con who couldn't lay a line of bricks
alongside me. It didn't matter that instructors earned fifteen
cents a day while I was only making ten cents. What hurt
was the total refusal of the prison to acknowledge my skill. It
was plain and simple— a non-white was not to be in a position over white cons.

The lock-in trumpet blew and I lined up with the rest and
was marched to my cell. Then I felt something clinging to my
fingers. It was the dandelion. I shook my head. *Didn't mean
to take you from your life.* I poured a little water into a small
mayonnaise jar, placed the flower gently in it, and stared at
it for a long while. It looked so goddamn lonely and out of
place in that plain old jar. From under my bed, I pulled out a
shoe box that contained what I needed. I went to work, and
in a short while the mayonnaise jar was painted a bright red
that heightened the dandelion's *chévere* yellow color. I lay
back on my bed and admired it.

"Hey, man, want some hot water?" It was a trusty.

"Yeah, thanks." I made hot tea and drank it in little sips,
having carefully laid out the tea bag to dry for next time.
Like it was only a tea bag, but it still had a long way to go
before it wasn't good for anything anymore.

I leaned against the bars of my cell, sipping my tea and

looking out over the walls. *The sky's having itself a sunset.* The orange-red slowly gave way to shades of purple, violet, and blue. I thought about cons who because of their own inner agonies put down others for trying. *I'm not the only one who's gotten sounded for digging book learning. Look at Gordo.*

Gordo, who was older and without much education, felt embarrassed at taking advantage of what little schooling was available. It was tough going to classes with cons who were young enough to be his kids. Like maybe he was afraid his lack of knowledge would show in class and he'd be laughed at by the kid-cons. It's damn tough to be laughed at as a kid, but as a man of forty or so? *Shit! I wouldn't feel too bad, Gordo.* There should be some way for older cons and kid-cons to be able to go to classes with their peers—and, for that matter, to do time with their peers. *This place has got rehabilitation down pat, on paper. Even when there ain't no kind of hope in sight, we gotta fight, man, we gotta fight.*

"Hey, you got salt for Bayamon?" a trusty asked.

"Yeah, here."

"Here's a sandwich for you. Bayamon sent it."

"Thanks."

I opened the toilet-paper wrapping and ate slowly.

"Hey, Piri," Bayamon's voice came echoing. "Thanks for the salt."

"No sweat. Thanks for the sandwich."

"It's a sardine with onions."

"Yeah, I know. Good looking out."

I washed my face, brushed the onion taste away with Colgate, and flopped heavily on my bed.

I heard some rapping on bars, that kind of noise only produced by a guard sliding his nightstick across them. It was always irritating. It was done to get us up in the morning and to tell us what time to eat, to keep quiet, to sleep. Nightstick rapping was one and the same with the lock-in-lockout trumpet signals. Yeah, like we were mice conditioned to signals for every action. The word was "acclimated." *Watch out! Buy that crap and there's no way to walk on earth as a man ever again.*

My thoughts went back to the letter I had sent to the Parole Board. I should have written it differently, and I dug myself rewriting it inside my head:

Mr. Alfred R. Loos
Chairman, Parole Board
Albany #1, Box 1679
New York, New York

DEAR SIR:

I am writing this letter regarding your decision in my case. I appeared before you on the August 27, 1953 Board and was given two years' Reconsideration Only.

I want you and the rest of the Board to know that I went up before you with a whole lot of expectation of getting cut loose on parole. When I first came into prison, I was given a whole lot of orientation on how I must either serve time or let time serve me. That if I chose, I could take advantage of everything that was at hand for rehabilitation and, believe me, that ain't much. But whatever little bit was there, I took advantage of. Anything and everything that I figured had some sense of positiveness to it, like from reading, brick masonry, etc. Yet, when I appeared before you, you didn't ask me what I had done with my time that was positive. Nay, like you jumped on my outside record and tried me all over again.

One of you even said, "You don't think you're going anywhere, do you?" Somebody else said, "Who do you think you are, Jesse James?"

Yeah, it was like being tried for what I had done outside and not for what I had been achieving inside.

Angry? You're damn right I'm angry. 'Cause the shit that's put down is that we are all sent to prison to pay a debt to society and that we are to be rehabilitated. Diggit. I just feel that we are put here not to be rehabilitated, but to have revenge taken against us.

Okay, if a man doesn't try, that's one thing. But if he tries, that's something else. There ain't no way to think a man's rehabilitated if all that's being poured on him is more hate, more inequities, more taking away of his sense of manhood and dignity.

I sure as hell wish you members of the Board would serve some time without nobody knowing you were members of the Parole Board, so that you could see, feel, and hear the sights, touch, and sounds of everyday prison tension filled with agonies. Like, we're supposed to be turned out back into society as functional human beings. No way. With the kind of racism and other sweats the con lives with in prison, the majority of us are gonna go out into the streets something else.

Man, most of us come in as so-called criminals and will be going out monsters.

Why don't you gentlemen take off your pinstriped suits and put on some prison grays and come live among us and dig what's happening, and you'd really get a firsthand, living view. You must, of course, change your ethnic views and racist views from white to black and brown, and when you'd all get back behind that big long table to make fast rulings on our lives, you'd be in a better position to make decisions.

Don't use these goddamn jailhouses for revenge, 'cause a lot of us will wait impatiently for our time to come, and go outside rehabilitated all right. But for the worst.

You can't strip us of our humanity and then turn us loose.

You all ain't got a right to create time bombs in prison and then turn us loose to blow up on the outside, not to mention inside here, too. Diggit.

Yours truly,
John P. Thomas

I smiled at the mental letter and knew if I had sent it, I would have pulled every bit of my fifteen-year maximum, if I survived that long.

I got out the letter I had really written and read it.

...When I appeared before you and the members of the Board, I had the intention of explaining myself clearly, but failed very badly and gagged up instead...

I am truly sorry for the hurt and misery I have caused

innocent people, my family included...There will always be the bitter memories in the lives of those whom I have hurt by my vicious crimes.

Even when I was caught, I still had the idea of being a tough guy and not caring. Yet when I arrived in this prison I began to take stock of myself. My Chaplain, Rev. Winch, called me in for an interview and I was distrustful of him and sullen, yet...day by day I was asking myself questions. Where am I going? What the heck am I doing with my life?

Rev. Winch would listen to me; he would hear my problems and advise me. I grew to trust and admire him. To him I was a young fellow. That's what he would call me.

I went before Mr. Burnott, the Educational Supervisor, and he led me to the trade of brick masonry. I took the course and graduated with 2,300 hours under my belt. I am now a pretty fair mason, lacking only actual working experience such as might be found on the outside.

I also took up a hobby, which was guitar playing, and I took a high school test and received a diploma from high school. I was trying to change my outlook on life.

Mr. Loos, all these things you and the members of the Board know...I am trying very hard to make a responsible man out of myself, a man who can be an asset instead of a drawback.

I'd like to be free; I would lie if I said I didn't mind being in prison...

You said that the brutalness of my crimes put something at fault with my makeup...You were right, sir, and yet, without wishing to contradict you, I would like to say it applied to a boy who considered himself a big shot, a very cool fellow, one who thought of himself as flying high...

I did these things the same way I drank whiskey and wine, smoked reefers, and sniffed heroin and cocaine...These things I did so as not to be considered a square, so as not to be considered a goody-good boy. At the time I believed the important thing was to be accepted, and with the crowd I hung with, it had to be this way...A little remark like, "Whatta you getting, cold feet?" Or, "Are you chicken?" or words like that would cause me to growl, "Are you kidding?" and off I would go...

I don't know, Mr. Loos, but that was me, afraid of being left out. Afraid of being a punk (which I now see I was anyway)...I'm trying to show that the boy who committed those crazy, brutal acts was not before you at the Parole Board, but a man who was trying to express himself, who failed because his crimes, when read to him, struck him in his face with disgust and shame. I gagged when my crimes were read off to me. I felt the disgust in your voice and when you spoke of my vicious crime against the old man, I felt as if I did not deserve to be called a man, a human.

I'd like to see my people proud of me. My Dad has never forgiven me. I have shattered his faith in me...I come from a good family. They are church-going people. Not one of them has had a police record...I must do all I can till I die to prove that the boy was father to the man in the true sense of the word...

I've got to show I have what it takes. I've stayed out of trouble here in prison. I can do the same outside, with God's help. Yes, I believe in Him, I've cause to.

Thank you, sir, for the time you have given me in reading this letter. Thank you for your consideration.

I remain,
Respectfully,
JOHN THOMAS #18193

Oh, shit, I thought, *it's the only way they'll listen to what I had to say without chancing pulling all my time.* I folded it carefully and put it away with my other treasures, my letters from home, and lay back to smoke a Pall Mall. I listened to the cellblock noise give way to silence as the trumpet blew and my mind turned off the rapping of the guards' sticks from here and there. After a while, the lights in all the cells went out.

I put on my earphones and listened to the disc jockey William B. Williams. He was playing "Blue Moon." *Oh, man, wonder what's happening on 104th Street in El Barrio?*

MUTTERINGS OF REBELLION

I sat in the mess hall, a little tired from laying those heavy cement blocks at ten cents a day. I stared at the few pieces of baloney and potato salad on my metal plate and began to eat quietly, lost in thought. The half-raw potatoes interrupted whatever was passing through my mind with the crunching sound they made as my teeth tried to mash them. I vaguely watched other cons coming in from their different labors and wondered if I should go out in the yard or line up and go to my cell. Through the giant, barred mess hall windows I saw that the day was sunny, so I decided I'd go out and get into a handball game.

I nodded at some greetings from *amigo* cons and let my mind run on how short I was. Like somehow August, 1953, had inched by and it was now July, 1955—only two more months till September, when I'd be sweating one mo' time before the Gods on Mount Olympus, alias the Parole Board.

I made a face as I swallowed, *God Almighty, that raw potato salad tastes like pure starch.* Someone sat down across from me—it was Johnny Lee. I glanced at him and noticed he had a bruise on the side of his face. It glared out in contrast to his white skin, puffed with a bluish redness that could only have come from a knuckle sandwich. I attempted a friendly smile while trying to suck out a small piece of raw potato that had gotten jammed in a cavity. Johnny Lee smiled grimly at me.

"You get lucky enough to run in an open cell gate, *amigo?*"

"Ain't none of your fucking business, buddy," Johnny Lee said, munching on his potato salad.

"Your potatoes raw, too?" I asked, quickly changing the topic.

"Ain't they always?" he grunted.

I shrugged my shoulders, and my expression told him I had no intention of putting myself in a position to become his whipping post. I went back to crunching and checking out cons and hacks, and trying to set to rhythm the banging of metal utensils that echoed through the great mess hall.

"Sorry, man." Johnny Lee was half-smiling at me.

"What for, man?" I said. "You ain't done nothing to me." I winked at him.

"I just got into a hassle." His voice sounded low and damn angry.

"Hey, *amigo*, you don't have to tell me nothing," I said, and went on inspecting my raw potatoes.

Johnny Lee nodded his head but ignored my words.

"Them sonofabitches," he went on, "with all the rest of the bullshit that's going on in here, they're still hanging on to their own prejudice crap."

I just nodded. He had the floor and interruptions were not in order, though I felt like asking if the lumps on his face were from cons or hacks, or both.

"That crud called me a spic-nigger lover because I hang around with you guys."

I nodded in understanding 'cause I'd heard, seen, and felt that *mierda* many times before and without a doubt would many more times to come. I dug his Caucasian face.

"Jesus Christ!" He gingerly touched the side of his face and his voice got angrier. "Yesterday I went over to the north wall to get into a handball game"—that was the white con- victs' wall and their almost unbreachable personal handball courts—"and this stupid sonofabitch"—Johnny Lee shook his head as if on the verge of a fit—"tells me to get over to the nigger wall where I belong. And the rest of them ignorant assholes with him fell all over themselves with this weak shit of 'We don't want you giving us a bad name. You wanna hang out with coons and spics, that's your business, but as far as we're concerned you're one of them.' Goddammit! I started to walk away after telling them to shove the wall up their asses, when one loud-mouth busted his dick string by yelling out that there was no doubt, either my Mom or Pop was a nigger, if not both."

I just nodded again. Johnny Lee held up a swollen right hand and said, "I hope to hell I busted his jaw. I'da done more except two other S.O.B.'s racked up some points on my face. Damnit, I hang around with whoever I want. Ain't nobody gonna tell me who my friends gotta be."

There was silence for a while. The last of my raw potatoes were now a part of my system. I looked at Johnny Lee and for lack of something to say I vaguely asked, "How come you didn't get busted, no hacks around?" I made a sandwich out of my baloney, wrapped it in a clean handkerchief, and put it in my swag bag.

"Yeah, them blue-coats came and busted it up, and them S.O.B.'s convinced the hacks we were just horsing around, body-punching. The S.O.B. I punched took a hack to the side and ten-to-one he told him a spic-nigger lover was being taught the error of his ways, and the hacks probably decided against busting me since the other guys had to be busted, too."

"Ain't the first time this shit's happened, Johnny Lee," I said with a deadpan face.

"I know, I know. But fuck it for glory, I got my right to hang out with whoever I want to."

"Ain't nothing wrong with that, Johnny, nothing wrong at all." I sucked the piece of raw potato out of my cavity.

"Christ Almighty," Johnny Lee swallowed hard, "these potatoes are really fucking raw."

"Yeah, ain't they?" I got up, picked up my tray, and smiled. "See you around, Johnny."

"Hey," he gestured, "wait a couple of minutes till I down the rest of this garbage and we'll play us a couple games of handball."

"Sure, why not?" I sat back down and we smiled kind of

knowingly at each other.

Ten minutes later Johnny Lee and I were at the handball court on the east wall. As we approached, I dug Pancho and Zorro playing against Gordo and Bimbo. The rest of us stood around waiting our turn to play the winners. Pancho and Zorro lost and two others took their places. Pancho came up to us; the sweat pouring off his face made his dark skin shine brightly. The sun was out, but the air was chilly.

"Hey, *panins*, what's happening?" Zorro smiled.

"Same old crap," I answered.

"Whew! Enough handball for me," Zorro said, wiping his face. "Can't put out energy from that shit they handed out in the mess hall for dinner."

"Christ, I'd damn near give my soul for some good home-cooked food," L'il Henry agreed. "Like nothing special—maybe some smothered pork chops and candied yams. Or even some plain poor folks' grit, like ham hocks with black-eye peas and collard greens." His face went through all kinds of appreciative changes as he continued. "And a ton of corn bread wrapped around tons of butter."

"Don't forget chitlins," laughed Pancho.

"Yeah, that too."

"How about some watermelon?" cracked Bayamon.

"Yeah, that too, motherfucker." L'il Henry grinned, almost ignoring the put-down. "How about that glob we get from time to time—they call it 'Spanish rice.'"

Bayamon slapped skin with L'il Henry.

"Man, they let me into that kitchen and I'd show them how to whip up some *alma* food in a *min-new-toe*. Like *arroz con pollo*, or *lechón asado*, or..."

I let the conversation become a blurred droning in my ears as my eyes roamed at will inside the yard. *There's something funny about today.* I couldn't quite make it out, but every pore on my body felt changes going on in the yard. Then I noticed some younger cons moving from group to group. They talked guardedly, and some heads shook no while other heads nodded yes.

"Hey, it's our turn, Piri," Johnny Lee broke into my

thoughts.

I went out to work up a sweat, and the strange feeling ducked out of my mind. I put it down to overdoing time.

"Let's get these cats," urged Johnny Lee, and we played hard against Gordo and Bimbo, determined to come out kings of the court. In no time at all we were standing on the sidelines. Gordo and Bimbo were red-hot. I blamed our defeat on the raw potatoes—why not? They hadn't tasted good enough to be anything better than scapegoats.

There was a hushed conversion going on, and Pancho and Bayamon were part of it. Pancho was shaking his head from side to side as I walked up in time to hear him say, "You cats are crazy. Man, that shit won't work."

"What's happening?" I asked, noticing a few cats, both Puerto Rican and black, who, although friendly, were not of our clique.

"They want to pull a strike," whispered Bayamon. "We're telling them it ain't gonna work."

"Why not?" said a grim-faced kid-con about eighteen or nineteen years old. "Why won't it work? We stage a sit-down strike and demand to see the governor for better changes in this fucking prison."

"It ain't gonna work 'cause it's not planned. Shit, you'd need at least the majority of the prison population. You'd need time to get the word around," argued Pancho.

"That's too dangerous, man," broke in a young Puerto Rican named Pulpo. "Chances are some rat would get word back to the Man faster than quick shit."

"Not as dangerous as being hung out in left field with just a handful of cons," Pancho countered. "And even with the majority, the end result might be better conditions. But one thing's sure—everybody involved gotta know they're in for some head-cracking, and maybe even getting killed. Uh-uh, count me out. This shit ain't planned good enough, let alone long enough."

"I feel that way, too," broke in Johnny Lee, ignoring some dark looks from the younger bloods. "You cats ain't thinking it all out. We should get us some organizers, set up committees, and cool-like, see if we can get the majority of us cons with the thing."

"We don't need you, you white motherfucker," a Negro chewed out.

"Ease off that shit, turkey," Pancho warned.

Johnny Lee turned a little red, but his voice was still calm. "Hey, man, maybe my skin ain't worth shit to you, but my life is. I got as much balls as you, even if they ain't black as yours." Johnny's voice took a rise.

"Ease off, you guys, Bayamon whispered. "Shit, that's part of our problem. You cats talk about getting the shit together and you can't even get yourselves together. Pulling all this together means just that—together. I was in a riot in Sing Sing, and you cats better believe it. You can pick up all the sticks and stones you want and do all kinds of numbers with your fists, but you better dig that it's gonna take more than heart to go against guards and state troopers and, diggit, even the armed forces if need be. They'd send planes in to strafe this fucking place if they had to. I'm in for the idea, but not for it coming out of thin air."

I hadn't said a word all this time.

"How about you, man?" It was me somebody was talking to.

Yeah, what about me? Like what the amigos are saying is right—this ain't planned no way at all. And besides, I got only two months to go.

"Say something, man. You ain't copping out, too, are you?" Pulpo's voice was *mucho* sarcastic. I opened my mouth but got interrupted.

"Hey, *hermano*, nobody's copping out," Pancho's voice glinted with angered patience. "If I'm gonna be part of something like this it's 'cause I want to do it, not because somebody's gonna pressure me into it. Diggit!"

I said nothing. My mind bubbled over, thinking on all the different fears I had lived with all my life. But I had survived in spite of them. I really felt I could do better on the outside. I knew damn well I could write—I could write about all this shit happening, about other things, too. *If only I can survive this place. Jesus, what's the use of jumping up on some soap-box in the middle of the prison yard to spout grievances? A few minutes at most and some hack'll jam his club down my throat. Like, who's to know what's happening here if nobody records it besides Warden and Company? Damn, if only it was better organized, that would be something else.*

"What do you think, Piri?" Now, Pancho pushed at me.

"If only it was better organized, that would be something else. It's like getting wasted for nothing, man. If it ain't done with a majority, the warden can always say it was just a few troublemakers doing a stupid number."

And Bayamon straightway added, "So if we can get this thing together, O.K., I got as much heart as anybody. But I got some brains to go with it, too. Pulpo, you or nobody else is gonna embarrass me into suicide by putting me down as a punk, *entiendes?*

The young cons walked away. Their under-the-breath mutterings weren't nice. I watched them walk away and they walked like boppers. No doubt they'd been busted for gang-fighting on the outside. *Heart is great, but without a mind, you're a vegetable.*

The trumpet blew and we trudged to our cells.

That night, Flaco, who had tried to make the playing-card bomb, blew his mind. He began laughing insanely in his cell, the sounds growing louder and louder without rhyme or reason. Flaco matched his hysteria with clapping palms as though at a Pentecostal meeting. He laughed and laughed, screamed and mumbled, and guards came running. He slammed his cell stool at the bars as if telling the hacks to go away, like his mental pain and madness were his own.

We could watch the scene on the tier below because it was reflected in the giant windows across from us. Flaco screamed a flood of obscenities that were almost prayer-like in their force and knelt in front of his toilet bowl, putting his arms around it. With the unbelievable strength that is born of madness, he strained and ripped it loose from its moorings. Toilet water cascaded over the tier to form a pool below.

More guards came and a barrage of tear gas was fired into his cell. Flaco went frantic, rubbing his eyes and coughing his anger out. The cell door was opened and blows began to fall like heavy rain. Flaco punched at empty air and hit the steel walls of his cell, but finally fell beneath the head-busting sticks and sprawled in the toilet water on the cell floor.

We watched as they pulled him from his cell. His prison shoes dragged toe-downward and his arms scrapped the cold steel floor of the tier. I heard the *bumpety-bump* as he was dragged down the stairs and from a strained view saw a little piece of him being forced into a strait-jacket. He was taken away to solitary, his face contorted in a portrait of anguish. *So death is not just dying.*

The next morning the droplets of dried blood blazed a trail to the box. The facial muscles of the guards were impassive. Our facial muscles were most uptight. It was hard to look at a hack and not think of violence.

One more time: *Rehabilitation, my ass!*

FELIZ CUMPLEAÑOS

I adjusted the collar on my heavy gray prison jacket and trudged to the stands. It was a cold, overcast September day and the frozen grass beneath my boots cracked as it was forced to accept my weight. I saw Pancho, L'il Henry, Bayamon, Santurce, and the rest of our clique huddled around two green metal tables that had been put together to form a setting for some thermos bottles and two cakes.

"Hey, here's Piri. Hey, brother, just in time," greeted Bayamon.

"What's happening?" I gestured a hello to everybody and dug the cloud of frosted breath coming out of all of us.

"It's a party, man," smiled Pancho. "These turkeys went and sprung a surprise birthday party for you and me. Diggit, *panín*."

I dug it, and sure enough it was two prison-made birthday cakes with writing on them. One read HAPPY BIRTHDAY, PIRI—*Four Years Old*. The other HAPPY BIRTHDAY, PANCHO—*Four Years Old*.

I smiled, feeling pleased, and got a little out of voice 'cause this seemed such an unnatural place to have such a natural thing as a birthday party.

"Ain't these guys something?" Pancho was grinning with sincere appreciation.

I studied the cakes. "Yeah, but what do you guys mean 'Happy Birthday...Four Years Old'? Like I'm twenty-six years old this month."

"Ain't you got no sense of humor, brother?" L'il Henry said. "That's how long you've been in."

"Yeah." said Bayamon. "Like it's one way of spitting in

Time's eye."

"Some fucking sense of humor," I said a little grimly. "Ain't *nada* happy about these goddamn four years."

"Hey, fucko—you ain't gonna spoil our birthday party, are you?" Pancho squinted a good-natured evil eye at me.

"Nay, *nunca*." I laughed and looked each one of my *amigo*-con-brothers dead in the eye, and with untainted sincerity said, "Diggit, fellas, this is really beautiful of you cats. *Gracias*."

"Yeah," Pancho added. "Good looking out, thanks," and for a split second of time there were no words said; just an awkward silence of clearing throats entwined with some sort of understood embarrassment.

Santurce came up to Pancho and me, and with a smile that almost made his face disappear, handed us each a rolled-up piece of heavy drawing paper.

"Happy Birthday, Pancho. Happy Birthday, Piri."

Pancho and I mumbled our thanks and rolled open the gifts. I stared at the drawing on mine. There was no doubt about Santurce's artistic abilities.

"Goddamn, this is beautiful," Pancho said.

"It's the rain forest on top of El Yunque," grinned Santurce.

I dug my gift. "This can't be no other place except El Morro Castle, right, Santurce?"

"That's right, *hermano*. How come you know that shit and you ain't never been to P.R.?"

"Damn, man," I smiled. "They make picture postcards of Puerto Rico." I slapped skin with Santurce. "All shit aside, *panín*, this is beautiful. Diggit, you're good."

Santurce gestured away my praise with a flick of his hand, but put on a couple of inches of pleased pride to his height.

"*Caramba*," Pancho studied his drawing. "Just looking at this scene—wow." He shook his head almost sadly. "I can't wait to see Puerto Rico again." And looking at the scene of El Morro in my hands, he said, "You ought to go there when you get a chance, Piri. It's like *nada* else."

"Yeah," I nodded my head thoughtfully in agreement, "I ain't never been there, all right. Kinda like *mi madre* used to talk up a storm about the island. You know, stuff about how beautiful it was, with all them *chévere* beaches and mountains, all different *frutas*, and all the sunshine one could stand. Yeah, Pancho, Puerto Rico is on my agenda."

"What's that mean? You and your big words."

"*Agenda*, ignoramus, means it's on my list of things to do."

Pancho looked about seriously, and in a solemn voice declared, "Mark my *palabras*, fellas. This *hombre* is going to go a long way. Anybody that can master words like 'con-glom-er-a-tion' and 'man-i-fes-ta-tion' can do anything with his agenda."

We all cracked up, though it was at my expense. It was like coming from a family.

Bayamon put the candles on both cakes. "Hope these cakes taste good. We had to lay out four cartons of tailor-made smokes for them. Christ, what a hype—them *blancos* in the bakeshop sure got it made."

"Hey, don't spoil this good old party," L'il Henry broke in. "What's the difference what we paid? It's worth it. Fuck it!"

Bayamon rubbed his nose and, talking to the cakes, answered, "You're right, Henry. It's just them cons splitting us from our hard-earned loot so easy gripes the shit outta me, and...."

He stopped talking and lit the candles.

Santurce began to sing "Happy Birthday" in Spanish:

> *Feliz Cumpleaños a ti,*
> *Feliz Cumpleaños a ti.*

Gordo cut him off. "Aw, cut that weak shit out. Whatta you think this is, some fucking kid's birthday party?"

I dug Pancho's eyes were somewhere else and followed their direction. They were resting on the person of Siegfried the hack, who stood observing us with a shit-eating half-smile on his face, like he was amused at watching some gray-furred animals in a zoo play at being human beings. The rest of our fellers caught the vibrations from us and dug Siegfried's amusement. Gordo stopped making funny faces at Santurce for his singing and, nodding to us, gently began singing "Happy Birthday." All of us joined in, even Pancho and me:

> *Feliz Cumpleaños a ti,*
> *Feliz Cumpleaños a ti,*
> *Feliz Cumpleaños a Pancho y Piri,*
> *Feliz Cumpleaños a ti.*

We stared at Siegfried. He stared at us. He shook his head as if in some secret joke and turned away to pry into somebody else's business.

"Ain't you gonna blow out the candles?" Santurce interjected.

Pancho and I smiled at him and between us we blew away eight years' worth of time. We cut into the cakes with a twelve-inch wooden ruler—like nohow were knives allowed—and exploded into laughter when, childlike, Santurce asked, "Hey, ain't you guys gonna make a wish?" Nobody had the heart to tell him to "cut that weak shit out." Not even Gordo.

KANGAROO COURT

I had signed up for some Bible studies given by the prison chaplain, Rev. Claude V. Finch, and it was time for class. I showed the construction guard my pass. He stared at it and nodded an O.K. I left my tools clean, washed myself up, and walked down the hall, stopping to show my pass to whichever guard demanded it. I entered the classroom and sat down with the dozen or so other convicts who were about to spend an hour listening to "Rev." Winch expound on God, Christ, and Christianity.

My mind turned off what I felt wasn't relevant to me and absorbed what was, most especially his thoughts on the power of positive thinking. He offered for loan a book that had been written by someone named Norman Vincent Peale. I raised my hand first and copped the book. *Something positive in the negative atmosphere.* My mind got lost in one of its frequent trips to the outside world, and the pros and cons of the conversation around me melted into the background. Suddenly I was nudged by the inmate next to me. I came back to serving time.

"Yeah, what is it?" I mumbled to him.

"The chaplain asked you a question," he said, smiling.

"Sorry, Chaplain, I wasn't here for the moment. What did you ask?"

The chaplain studied me for a second, smiled, and repeated himself. "I said, 'Do you believe that a man can put old things aside, like a past negative life, and erect a new life for himself with a total, positive outlook?'"

"Yeah, if he's strong enough in his heart and mind. I mean strong enough to shut out all this shit. Sorry,

Chaplain."

"No sweat, I've heard the word before."

I nodded soberly and went on, "All this shit going on around him. I guess it's like that guy Paul said in the Bible, about when he was a child he acted like a child, and now that he was a man he was putting all childish things aside, or something like that. But, er, aw, Hell!"

"Yes, go on."

"I don't think it's us cons that gotta be positive alone. It's the rest of the so-called good guys, too."

"Yeah, like hacks," came a voice. There was some laughter.

"You're right, son. Everybody—starting with me—too."

The chaplain asked another con a question and I flew back to the streets with my mind. The signal blew for the end of the session. *Time to split to wherever we came from.*

Norman Vincent Peale's book somehow felt heavy under my arm as I walked out of the classroom. I couldn't help musing that whatever writings about positive thinking he had put between the book covers worked only for others like him in this world. *But it's funny how people think 'cause we're cons we can't think positive for ourselves. Aw, let me check the cat's book out.*

I felt Rev. Winch's hand on my shoulder.

"How's it going, Tommy?"

I grinned, thinking of how he had latched on to my last name and made a tag out of it.

"O.K., Chaplain, O.K."

"Remember what I've told you many times. Don't let getting hit with two more years blur your mind."

I nodded and walked on, wondering how he expected me to perform the miracle of seeing completely crystal clear through the damn muck and mire of prison existence. *But I'll make damn sure to see clearly enough to make it through.* No way was I going to die in prison for nothing except to rest at last on a hill outside the wall under a stick with a number painted on it. My feet led me out to the prison yard where a guard challenged me and I held up my pass. Out of force of habit, he passed me through without looking at it. I sat on the edge of a concrete curb and idly watched cons walking around. The cold air felt good. I became aware of the pressure of the book under my arm, opened it, and began to read at random.

"Number 18193...Number 18193...report to the cellblock front desk. Number 18193, report at once."

Damn, that's me...Don't tell me I'm getting a surprise visit. It's been a long time since la familia's *come up to see me. Maybe it's Tía Angelina.* I remembered how Tía hadn't liked the town of Comstock. She told me that the people were very unfriendly, especially if they knew one was coming to visit *el Presidio.* I dug that she had meant they were prejudiced. I didn't even tell her how much more so they were inside the walls.

"Number 18193, report at once to the cell hall front desk."

If it was a surprise visit, I didn't want to waste one second of it. *Put down shoe leather and pick up gravel real fast!* I got up to the front desk puffing out cold air and nodded at the Sergeant in the glass-and-wood section.

"I'm 18193." *That's not my rightful name.*

"Just stand there," the Sergeant said.

"Do I have a visit?" I asked.

"Just stand there," he repeated.

I stood, and a minute or so later the construction hack, Wardell, came into view. He walked up to me and said, "Where the hell do you think you're supposed to be at this time?"

And then it hit me—I wasn't supposed to be in the yard at this time. I was supposed to be back laying cement blocks at ten cents a day, to be on close terms with my trowel and level. *Where was my head at when I walked out into the yard and felt the fresh, cold air like I had the right?*

"What—*what* did you think you were doing?" His voice wasn't angry, it wasn't happy, it was just a cold, matter-of-fact hack voice.

"I got lost in thought and just found myself in the yard. I wasn't trying to escape." I felt the skin on my jawbone get tight and grow dry. It would be his word against mine before a kangaroo court made up of his peers, and getting an attempted escape bullshit conviction on your record was good for added time. "But your actions could be so construed. I got my job to do and you got yours, and yours is to be where you're supposed to be when you're supposed to be. Let's go." Wardell turned to the Sergeant. "Gimme a keep-lock sign." The Sergeant handed him a tin sign similar to the one at Sing Sing. Three inches high and twelve inches long, it was neatly painted in red capital letters: KEEP LOCK.

"Let's go."

I muttered something under my breath.

"What did you say?" His voice took on a warning sound.

"I said I wasn't trying to escape and that this is a jive bust."

"We'll see. Let's go."

I led the way and stepped into my cell. He turned the large key and then interwove the keep-lock sign between the bars of my cell to notify the next shift that I wasn't to be let out until further notice.

"How long do I stay here?" I said to the bars.

"You'll be going to court. They'll let you know how long." Wardell gave a tug on a steel bar and, satisfied it wasn't going nowhere, split. I stared at the sound of his going-away soles and heels and broke into a smile at the book still in my hands: *The Power of Positive Thinking*, by Dr. Norman Vincent Peale.

A few hours later, the rest of the construction gang came in for lockup. Bayamon checked out my keep-lock sign.

"What you get busted for?" he grinned kindly.

"For thinking I was a civilian," I smiled back.

"What?" He looked quizzically at me.

"I took a walk into the yard instead of going back to work after a positive bull session with the chaplain."

"Hey, *amigo*, better watch yourself. You can't be forgetting where you're at."

"You're telling me."

"Hey, you—it was Wardell the hack's voice—"stop bullshitting with that keep-lock or you'll join him. Get into your damn cell."

"Jesus," whispered Bayamon, "I'd like to lay a couple of cement blocks inside his fucking mouth."

"Just make sure they're level, baby. You gotta take pride in your work, Mr. Brick Mason, *mucho* pride."

"Later, man. Good luck in court."

"Yeah." I plunked on my bed, stretched out, and put on my earphones. I heard Wardell's feet coming my way, and just before his shadow came into view, I shut my eyes, giving him my own keep-lock. He made the rounds, locking cell door after cell door, and ten minutes later there wasn't a hack on the tier. Pancho rapped on his wall and the rap came into my cell.

"Yeah, what's happening?"

"Bayamon is calling you." I lifted one end of my earphones from my head and whispered, "What is it?"

"I'll see you in court, man. That *hijo de la gran puta* gave me a keep-lock on 'general principles,' to quote that sonofabitch."

The occupants of a whole lot of cells broke out in laughter at Bayamon's misfortune, with the exception of me; and then even I laughed. Like, sometimes it's true— misery does love company.

The next day I tried to shut out the surroundings of my cell by reading, sleeping, or just plain thinking. Some footsteps came up the tier and stopped in front of my cell.

"What happened, Tommy? Pancho told me you were keep-locked." I stared at Rev. Winch. He was a tall, lean, white-haired, white-skinned man at least sixty years old.

"Ah, it's strictly a jive bust, Chaplain. The hacks talked some shit about it possibly being an attempted escape. Imagine that crap—and me just sitting in the yard reading a book on positive thinking."

"Well, escape I'm sure it isn't." He was serious.

"No, that wasn't in my mind. But you ought to know, there ain't one con that don't think about it one time or another—yours truly included."

"Well, I checked. You'll be going to court sometime today. I'll be there to help any way I can."

I felt like telling the chaplain not to bother 'cause he'd be wasting his time, but it was kind of hard to down a man who's trying to help, so I just said softly, "Good looking out, Chaplain. I appreciate it."

As he walked away, my mind jumped out with the thought, *Diggit, a man like that can just about keep a cat from totally believing that his God doesn't exist. Like his God is real for him. Where the hell is mine?*

I stood outside the Principal Keeper's office. A half-dozen or so other inmates, including Bayamon, waited along with me for their day in court. There was no talking among us— the guards had ordered silence. Cons went in and cons came out. My number was called and I was ushered into a room where, behind a table, sat several blue-uniformed high officers.

"Your number?" said one.

"Number 18193, *sir*."

"Do you suffer from loss of memory?" said another.

"No, sir."

"So why didn't you report back to your work gang after your meeting instead of taking a walk in the yard?"

"Dunno," I answered. "I guess my mind was thinking over what I had learned in class."

"It could have been thinking escape," said another voice.

"Sitting in the yard, reading a book, sir?" I replied. "I wasn't thinking that..." and added, "*sir*."

I heard the chaplain's voice.

"This inmate's got a pretty fair record, Principal Keeper, and he's getting short. It happens sometimes that a man can get disoriented. I'm sure his actions weren't intentional."

"Umm," said a voice. "It would seem that after four years or so, a man would know what to do or not to do as far as rules and regulations go." Turning to me, "If you eventually want to leave this place, you're going about it the wrong way. If this happens again..." The thought was left hanging. I started to say something in my defense, man to man, but killed the idea faster than stepping on a cockroach. *He means, if this happens again, it'll go down as attempted escape.*

Damn, my mind could come up with thoughts at a moment's notice, no matter where. And right there in front of the kangaroo court I found myself thinking what a bone-crushing disappointment these white, supposedly Christian beings would suffer if at Judgment Day they found themselves face to face with God and he was Puerto Rican and black to boot.

I watched as one of the kangaroo judges wrote something down. Looking up at me he said flatly, "Don't let me see you before us again for the same infraction. For this one, punishment will be two weeks' yard and movie privileges taken away. Also, no earphones in your cell for the period designated. You'll go to work and back to your cell."

I opened my mouth to protest how heavy the court was being for such a small bullshit offense when another judge added, "Unless you'd rather not go to work and spend the two weeks completely locked up in your cell."

I kept quiet. *Two weeks in a toilet room? No thanks.* In fact, if I opened my mouth there was a damn good chance of the box and maybe a visit from some muscle-bound guards looking for a punching bag. *Diggit,* my brain told me, *remember them cats that went in the box and came out looking like shit on a shingle? Play the game,* papo, *play the game.*

"O.K., dismissed." I walked out under Wardell's escort. He locked me in.

"Maybe next time you'll know better." he prodded.

I smiled. "I already know better. Believe me, I do."

"Good. If you boys just learn the ropes, you'll never have any trouble."

I nodded, thankful he couldn't read my mind. My thoughts were positively negative.

"Let's have them." He reached an open hand through the cell bars. "Come on, gimme your earphones—no radio, remember?"

I coiled the long wire carefully around the earphones and handed them to him.

"You'll get them back when your time is up."

I laughed inside. I was doing time inside of doing time. Wardell shook his head. I guessed he was signifying that he could never understand us kind of people.

He went away and took my treasured earphones with him. I wondered how I could stand two weeks without the wisdom and cool sounds of William B. Williams or the stand-up, shoot'em-up courage of Marshal Dillon on "Gunsmoke." I stretched myself mightily and let out a repressed fart, not feeling one damn bit ashamed at the natural biological performance.

"Hey, *panín*." It was Bayamon.

"Yeah, Bro?" I answered back.

"Whatcha get, man?"

"Two weeks' loss of all privileges."

"Tough shit."

"What went down with you?" I asked.

"Three days for talking to a keep-lock—and a convict to boot."

"Are you sorry?" I laughed.

"Half and half," he laughed back.

"Fair enough, *panín*," I yelled. "At least half your heart's in the right place."

"Christ sake, you guys never learn." The voice came tearing down the tier. It was Wardell. "Don't you guys ever learn?"

I know me and Bayamon were bursting to tell him off, but kept quiet. Bayamon, like me, was probably grinding his teeth together and wishing we knew the secret of making voodoo dolls. Suddenly, a con's voice from two tiers below called out in falsetto tones, "Hey, Wardell, why don't you put a keep-lock on your old lady's snatch, seein' how you dig keep-locks so much?"

Wardell blew his cool in anger. "You sonofabitch. Say that to my face. You goddamn punk."

All he got back in reply was the long, squeaky, drawn-out

call of the asshole artists, and from the intensity of sound, it was a bouquet of nothing less than jailhouse orchids. My eyes hit on the calendar on my cell wall. It was getting close to the new year, 1955. *If I pull all my time to its maximum, what's the world outside gonna be like in 1965?*

IT'S A MATTER
OF DIGNITY

A prison riot explodes like a boiler that's built up steam from a long way back. When it comes, control is near impossible, especially if there's been no real planning, no prisoner unity, and only scattered, disorganized leadership.

Trouble that's coming got a way of showing its face. It's hard to overlook in a 360-degree mirror of impotent frustration. It's getting tired of seeing a fellow prisoner ground into the dust under a barrage of clubs for daring to stand up as a man in a verbal clash with a hack. It's the tiredness of time and again seeing many whites make parole the first time round while black and browns are held over.

The Comstock riot of August, 1955 began like other riots, a peaceful protest: communication with prison officials was attempted and grievances put forth. Those in power presented a deaf ear and met the cries against prison inequities with blows and abuses, arrogance, and sadistic reprisals.

There wasn't a day that passed at this time without some cons talking about breaking out or presenting grievances in written form or in verbal pleas to the prison officials—always to no avail.

For weeks, the prison war clouds had been gathering: an incident here, a lone action there, pushy hacks cursing cons only to be cursed right back, sullen disobedience to orders, and looks of undisguised defiance. Keep-lock signs were on many cells, and though locking in prisoners for refusing to work or talking on line wasn't too much out of the ordinary, and though over a thousand cons were not keep-locked, it was still handwriting on the wall.

Then one day in August, at around 5:00 P.M., hell broke loose with a thunder clap. The loudspeaker blared out repeatedly as over a hundred and fifty convicts stood defiantly by the west wall and refused to move. This was a spontaneous strike by a minority of inmates. The rest of us were herded to our cells under the watchful guns of the towers. The crisp air seemed suddenly to take on a deathlike chill and the abnormal silence that hung in the air between inmates and guards was fearful in its hostile intensity.

I could sense the struggle going on inside each inmate as we faced the decision of whether or not to tear loose from our lines and charge across to join the striking inmates huddled against the wall. No doubt this would have resulted in violence, for we were surrounded by guards in the yard and above us on the walls. We filed through this magic atmosphere without incident.

Since my cell faced the yard, I could see clearly all that was taking place outside. I pressed my forehead against the bars, grasping them tightly in my hands, and silently stared out into the big yard. It was like being in a theater digging heavy drama from the loge. The prisoners and guards looked almost unreal from the distance of one or two city blocks. I couldn't see faces clearly, but the gray clothing and blue uniforms left no doubt as to who was who.

Ultimatums to the striking inmates still blasted from the various loudspeakers, demanding the inmates give up their strike and allow themselves to be taken to their cells. I heard the promise of "no reprisals." Not one inmate made a move to accept, although I could see groups here and there huddled together in what I took to be councils. Leadership was being sought in the sparse time left them. A gray blur accompanied by two others approached the guards, who by this time had been reinforced by a multitude of heavily armed state troopers.

The inmates, under an improvised flag of truce, came up to the prison officials. Amidst angry gesturing from both sides, there was some apparent negotiation. The inmates turned and walked back to their wall. A last warning blared out and then a vacuum-like hush settled over the grassy space of the prison yard for a few moments that seemed hours long.

At a signal, the guards and troopers began to move toward the inmates. They advanced slowly at first, armed with rifles, tear gas, water hoses, clubs, and other weapons allotted them.

The inmates picked up rocks and tore down wooden stands for clubs, and almost to the man didn't move back an inch. Outnumbered and outgunned, they began to walk toward the guards and troopers approaching them. As the guards and troopers broke into a run, the inmates did the same.

What was missing—sound—suddenly exploded into being, a unified roar from both sides as they crashed together with the force of hate, anger, and frustration. The guards and troopers believed they were dealing with subhumans. I could see it in the carriage of their bodies and in the way they swung their clubs and rifle butts with deadly intent. The inmates met the onslaught manfully, but were swallowed up in an ocean of guards' blue and troopers' brown. Fighting was hand-to-hand. Gray bodies crumpled up and crashed limply on the green grass. The air was filled with screams and curses and a medley of orders being shouted on both sides.

The inmates fell back under the overwhelming crush, turned, retreated, rallied, but were charged again. In turn, they charged to meet the enemy. Christ Almighty! It was hopeless, but it had gut-ripping courage.

Inside the cellblock, a play-by-play description was being given to the cons whose cells did not face the yard, and the different versions seemed to turn the block into a barred Babel. The battle outside was suddenly dominated by the unmistakable sounds of gunfire. We wondered if the real slaughter had begun.

The fever of anger, fear, and helplessness spread like a flash flood through the cellblocks. Over a thousand of us locked-in inmates lifted our voices as one, and the sound thundered throughout the prison, reverberating in deafening echoes. We began to hit the walls and bars of our cells with our fists, stools, shoes, whatever was at hand. The noise of imprisoned anger was frightening, but at the same time provided a sense of unity and comradeship, not only between us, but also with those engaged in the terrible bloody battle in the prison yard.

Night fell and the struggling figures in the yard could be made out in the light of the search beams. Hours passed and still the sounds of rage from our throats did not diminish. Jars, cans, and whatever else could be thrown out of cells smashed through the interior prison windows to the flats below inside the prison building. Large wads of mattress stuffing, newspapers, and rags or clothing, all soaked in lighter fluid, were flung out of hundreds of cells. It seemed like a bastardized Fourth of July, both scary and beautiful, as objects swarmed through the air like shooting stars and burst on the concrete floors below where they hissed and fought to keep from going out.

At first, guards attempted to wet down the fiery missiles, but barrages of heavy cans of food discouraged their attempts. The smoke grew as heavy as the curses and hatred pervading the entire prison. Racial put-downs on both sides were rampant.

Guards kept noting down cells from which articles had been thrown and even cells where curious inmates merely stood by the bars, showed reason enough to go on the "shit list." The smell of tear gas was everywhere; the breeze that floated gently in from the outside had spread the gas evenly throughout the cellblocks. There wasn't a dry eye in the place. The prison had taken on all the aspects of Dante's Inferno.

By 3:00 the next morning, the strike had been broken. The inmates, using rocks, sticks, and fists, had been defeated by guards and troopers armed with water hoses, machine guns, tear gas, and rifles. The ensuing chaos was a nightmare. Screams and blood became one and the same. The beatings in cells went on for hours, for days. Word came through that the prison doctor had asked the guards not to bring any more beaten inmates to the hospital. He would attend to their wounds in their cells.

We heard reports of a guard captain breaking the arms of inmates over his knee the way a sword is snapped after a court-martial. We heard that the prisoners being transferred to a special section of the prison had to carry their mattresses on their heads, and that as they dropped their mattresses into the new cells, they were sent sprawling on top of them by a club to the back of the head.

These rumors spread through the cellblocks like the smell of tear gas. The fury of reprisal was a monster unleashed. The anguished cries of inmates in pain intermingled in a horrible rhythm with the clubs that beat on their bare flesh. Many inmates who had not participated in the strike, but who had at any time annoyed a guard, got broken heads and bruised bodies from surprise visits to their cells. It was the ideal opportunity for the guards to take care of past antagonisms.

The yard was a shambles. The inside of the prison was littered with the debris of flying missiles, the fiery comets that had blended with the sounds of broken jars coming from over a thousand cells. Unity for the strike had come at last, but it was too late. The majority of us inmates who were part of the struggle had allowed ourselves to be locked behind cell bars.

At one point, Siegfried, the guard with whom I had had a run-in, came to my cell to take care of business with me. As he began to open the gate, I calmly committed myself to rush him and go over the edge with him to a hard concrete floor three tiers below, hoping I'd have the luck to land on top and die not too badly smashed up. A decent guard saved me the trouble by pulling him away.

I felt totally helpless, locked in a cell suspended in Inferno. I could only stare at three solid walls and look through the opening of my cell bars, completely vulnerable. Siegfried had caused no fear within me. I was past that stage and whatever came I was of the mind to make my life count, even if only for a few minutes.

What really was tearing a hole in me was a profound sense of loneliness. We were all shadows in lonely cells. The cries and curses of inmates being beaten was something I couldn't turn off. What my ears drowned out, my sweating pores absorbed. *And still the walls had not come tumbling down.*

From time to time I'd hear footsteps nearing my cell. The sound was always threatening in its heaviness. I'd wait with a sense of expectation, betting against myself that it would be Siegfried again. He had such a determination to rearrange my body structure with his brown club. Only once was it him, and he just walked by without even blinking an eye.

I knew that many of my fellow inmates were in their cells feigning sleep or trying to conduct some semblance of routine cell business. I kept trying to think non-prison thoughts, but it all came out the same. The sounds...the hurting pains...the being buried alive in a cell.... Then I remembered an old black inmate named Bald who bred canaries.

Bald was a short, heavy-set man who had been in prison something like twenty-nine years, which was more than my whole lifetime. According to what he let out about his past, he had been a cab driver in Chicago during the Roaring Twenties, but had left town fast due to some trouble with the police over transporting bathtub gin in his cab. He had gone to New York and eventually been busted on a murder rap. He'd been imprisoned for the rest of his natural life.

Bald was what is commonly known as a jailhouse lawyer. He never ceased fighting his case. He had been in three different riots in three different prisons. One in Dannemora in the late thirties had almost been the end of him, for he barely survived a savage beating by the guards.

Bald had the dubious privilege of requesting transfers to a different prison every ten years or so, a privilege granted to all convicts serving life. It was thought to be conducive to sanity to change one's surroundings every so often.

Bald loved canaries and would have filled the prison with them, but the prison rules stated that an inmate could have only so many canaries in his cell. Bald had exceeded the limit and was giving some of the birds away. I got one. I had felt excited at having a pet. I had never before owned a canary and I enjoyed watching him in his cage as he hopped around, warbling his behind off. But the more I watched him as the days rolled on, the more I began to identify with him. He was dependent on me for his existence the same way I was on the prison system.

I contemplated my canary, whom I had named Piri II, and made a decision to turn him free. I opened his cell door and he became hysterical. He bounced, jumped, and flew around his cage, caught in the grip of nameless fear. I tried to whistle him to calmness, but no good—he continued to bash himself against the bars of his cage. I finally caught hold of him gently, and, stroking him softly, I felt his heart beating in total terror.

"Hey, cool it, bird. What you can't do for me, I'm doing for you. I'm going to set you free."

I took him to my cell bars and catapulted him toward free side. There was room for only one con at a time in my cell.

Piri II took off without even looking back. I watched him fly to the great windows facing the cells, perch for a moment on the open window sill, and take off. I hoped he had the sense to fly high and make it over the prison walls.

Some time later, Bald had asked me how the canary was doing. When I told him I had set him free, Bald shook his head sadly and quietly said, "Hell, man, you didn't set him free. You sent him to his death. That canary doesn't stand a chance outside his cage. Them other birds out there will kill him as soon as they see him. Canaries bred in cages haven't got what it takes to survive out there. They get too used to being caged."

Old Bald hadn't been talking just about canaries. I thought about home and it seemed so remote that I felt I had never had a home, and my father, mother, sister, and brothers had belonged to someone else. In prison there was no more room for self-pity than there had been on my ghetto streets.

I was brought from my reverie by a commotion that interwove with the dull thuds and agonized screams of the ongo-
ing beatings.

Down on the flats, the guards and troopers were bringing
in the vanquished inmates. I could see by using the windows
as a mirror and, when I thought it was safe, by putting my
hand mirror between the bars, but only at the risk of having
my arm broken by the club of some overzealous guard. What
I saw tightened up my guts so much it kept me from vomiting
at the sight of sheer brutality. The inmates were being
beaten onto the flats, drenched from the powerful battering
of water hoses, blood running from different parts of their
bodies, especially their heads and faces. Many attempted to
stand up straight in a show of dignity, but staggered and
swayed semi-consciously, too far gone even to ward off the
blows being rained on them at random.

Bodies were laid out in a long row and I didn't know if
they were ordered to lie that way or if they were dead or
unconscious. I found out later that they were all injured. The
gunfire had ricocheted off the prison walls and struck some
troopers, but to my knowledge no inmate was shot. When I
pulled in my mirror from between the bars, one thing stuck
in my mind: the methodical manner in which the prisoners
were beaten. It was cold, almost scientific. The wet smears on
the polished concrete floor of the flats had shone with blood. I
believe I was finally lulled to sleep by the monotone sounds of
the cruel beatings.

For days afterward, we were shut off from the world—no
earphones, no newspapers, no letters in or out, nothing
except tension, tiredness, and terror. I wished at times I
could go deaf and blind to shut out the sights and sounds of
this torment in concrete called "correctional institution."

Those who took part in the strike were segregated in one
part of the prison and had their hair completely shorn. Black,
white, or Puerto Rican, their bald heads identified them as
blood brothers in a cause that failed. But had it failed?

When the prison returned to a state of normalcy, I'd
catch glimpses of them in small groups, marching in lines of

two. Barefooted, hands clasped behind their heads, they shuffled to the prison court to be handed their punishment for participation in the uprising, be it more time for assault, no parole, or solitary confinement. Whatever it was to be, I watched as they marched silently under heavy guard, faces scarred, swollen, and grim, with a paleness to their complexions regardless of skin hue. Under threat of force, they were not allowed to look anywhere but straight ahead or to talk with anyone. Yet a few dared look where they wanted, dared to whisper, and dared even to smile with dignity.

The rest of the prison population acknowledged their courage, and there was some sort of pulsating shame deep within us for not having joined them at the west wall. Looking back, I believe that if the majority of inmates had joined in organizing the strike for prisoners' rights on that day in August, 1955, it would have been an Attica, sixteen years before.

The alleged leaders of the strike were shipped to other prisons, but as one youngblood defiantly said, "They're doing us a favor by spreading us around. Wherever they send us, we'll get the shit going on again. It's a matter of dignity."

❖

EPILOGUE

September, 1955 came and I sat before the Parole Board. While they shuffled through my record, fast-running thoughts filled my mind. *I committed the crime; I pulled those stickups. I'd stand up to that. But who's going to stand up and admit it was this country's racial and economic inequalities that forced so many of us to the brink of insanity, making our anger and frustration so great that we literally blew ourselves over the precipice into deep, dark whirlpools of drugs and crime? Racism was my mind and anger was my heart, and I fought in the only way I figured was left open to me.*

I looked at one of the members of the Parole Board and remembered his saying two years ago, "You don't think you're going anyplace, do you? Who the hell do you think you are, some kind of Jesse James?" This time he opened his mouth and said, "How'd you like to go home?" Someone else said, "You're going to be released to two armed robbery warrants in the Bronx." Another voice added, "You're fortunate you weren't involved in the riot." I stared at the last speaker's noncommittal expression; his meaning was clear enough. If I had been involved, I'd be pulling my full fifteen years.

I was released from Comstock in October, 1955, having yet to answer to two armed robbery warrants. I left prison the same way I had come, wearing handcuffs and escorted by New York City detectives. I was taken to a big police station in New York, fingerprinted and photographed and then lodged in the Bronx County Jail, where I spent six weeks or so awaiting disposition of the two charges against me.

I was given a suspended sentence of three to seven years

and placed on probation. I had to report to both a parole officer and a probation officer. I was to be a double-checked ex-con.

When the judge cut me loose, I turned and walked into my Aunt Angelina's arms. Between smiles and tears, she hugged me tight. I hugged back. When we finally walked out of that building, I took a deep breath and rubbed my wrists as if trying to get the weight of past handcuffs off them.

My heart and soul held every inch and every minute of Great Meadows Correctional Institution. Tía patted my back gently. I stretched a wide smile for her and hustled her to a hot dog stand. Shivering in the chilly wind, I bought us two hot dogs with mustard and onions, as well as two ice-cold Coca-Colas, and paid for them from my prison wages of ten cents a day. I munched and watched free life moving around me. I had a strange feeling that I might blink and find myself back in that hell-hole in a pretty little valley in upstate New York.

I swallowed the frankfurter down in three gulps and flooded my stomach with the soda. I couldn't help thinking how much better Coke tasted outside the walls.

I ain't never going back. I'll hold court in the street first. Only way they'll get me back in that shithouse is muerto.

I smiled at Tía, put my arm around her shoulders, and said, "Tía, let's go home, huh?" and we both did a fast split to the subway station a couple of cold blocks away.

❖

APPENDIX 1

According to accepted statistics, about 10 percent of persons imprisoned are "hard-core" criminals who require commitment to maximum-security prisons. I believe the other 90 percent can be successfully rehabilitated in settings other than behind gray concrete prison walls. But since we still have to deal with the reality of the prison system as it exists today, efforts must be made at rehabilitation inside the walls.

In the last ten years, over 300,000 men and women have been incarcerated in American prisons. They have been forcibly removed by the state from society to serve their time and, supposedly, to be rehabilitated. Instead, the majority come out with a doctorate in crime, hardened by an overdose of brutality, twisted by racism, or physically and emotionally scarred by forced homosexuality. As prisoners, they were compelled to live as numbers instead of humans, dressed in state-issued uniforms and controlled by armed guards who were often motivated by sadism and racism. Prison dehumanizes by its sheer waste of human potential and produces too many persons with hate-filled outlooks who come out far worse than when they entered.

The responsibility for genuine rehabilitation rests heavily on those in charge of our correctional institutions. It must be based first on respect for prisoners as human beings. Sensitivity training for both the keeper and the kept, decent productive programs in vocational and academic fields, and respect for prisoners' ethnic and cultural heritages would help dignify the persons behind bars.

Crime takes a terrible toll of American lives and property. So does war. Let's treat crime as war and remember that when prisoners are taken in times of war, the Geneva Convention provides assurances of humane treatment for enemy soldiers. What's wrong with according the same rights to American citizens who have been incarcerated? In wartime, committees from the Geneva Convention visit prisoner camps to inspect the conditions. What's wrong with doing the same thing in American prisons with committees made up of representatives of different ethnic backgrounds? Unfortunately it takes a prison riot such as the massacre at Attica in 1971 to arouse public awareness and concern. And then, when it is no longer newsworthy, the public too often forgets that there are still many thousands living in prisons under similar conditions.

Before prisoners are released, there should be a system to reintroduce them to society and gradually acclimate them to living on free side. This can be done through the establishment of halfway houses or weekend furloughs.

I believe that when an inmate has earned his or her good time and is eligible for parole, it should not be dependent on first securing employment. This system of parole, called "open date," requires an inmate to have a job guaranteed on the outside before release. I have seen hundreds of inmates writing literally thousands of letters seeking employment, to no avail. Very few employers on free side would even entertain the thought of hiring ex-cons via a letter, no matter how sincere or passionately it has been written. For many inmates, an open date of six months can stretch into two years or more of prison simply because their return address is a prison.

The great majority of those who get released by this system have had jobs set up by friends or relatives who actually pay the employer to cover the employee's salary. These inmates usually work a couple of family-paid weeks until they find employment more to their liking.

It's one thing to know you've been denied parole. It's a torment to know you have been granted parole and can't get out because you haven't got a job.

While I was in prison, I constantly savored the day I would taste freedom. I had all kinds of daydreams of what it would feel like on free side again. I felt I wouldn't mind the grayness of the ghetto, no matter how rundown and dilapidated the tenement houses were. It wouldn't matter to live in competition with hot and cold running cockroaches and king-sized rats. It wouldn't matter to be surrounded by oceans of human beings strung out on drugs and poverty. It would have to be better than doing time. After seven long years of hate, tension, and verbal and sometimes physical abuse, my mind said anything would be better. Whatever rehabilitation came to me, most of it came from other inmates and from myself.

Surviving in prison was like walking on a thin thread, a very delicate line of balance. If you had too much spirit, it would be challenged by the system and you stood a good chance of being physically and emotionally destroyed.

Rebels have always been a threat to the prison system. If you fought for your rights by rebelling against sub-human treatment, you put yourself on the prison's black-list as one who constituted a danger to the status quo. The system had to break you to the harness lest that spirit of dignity infect other prisoners who had become institutionalized.

If you were willing to cooperate with the prison system, either in an honest attempt at self-rehabilitation or in making a favorable impression when parole time rolled around, you were sure as hell going to be ostracized by fellow inmates and put down as an "ass-kisser," traitor, or, even worse, an informer. Whatever the reasons for cooperating, very few inmates were rewarded by the prison officials.

If you tried to play it ultra-cool by trying to avoid all trouble, you left yourself wide open as an easy mark. You were in danger of becoming a whipping post to be abused by anybody who hit on you.

I made it out of prison, but somewhere in my mind there's a twenty-mile-high granite tombstone with the carved numbers of inmates who fell victims of an inhuman prison system, sacrificed, slaughtered, to society's god of retribution.

Before I was released from prison, the authorities filled my head with all kinds of threats and warnings of what would happen to me if I stepped out of line on the outside and how in the twinkling of an eye I could be back in the slams. I was to be an ex-con on parole with few or no civil rights. If I had been a second-class citizen before I went to prison, and a third-class citizen in prison, I was a fourth-class citizen upon my release.

In 1955, when I was released, there were no organizations working with parolees, with the exception of the Police Department, the Department of Corrections, and some religious groups. Parolees come out of prison badly shook-up, scared on the inside even if they didn't show it. Very few can re-enter society with no sweat at all. It is a process that takes determination, time, and *mucho* patience. There is a high rate of recidivism because it is hard to make it on the outside. Face it, when jobs are hard to get on free side for non-offenders, being non-white and an ex-con makes it near impossible. Don't care who you are. You've got to eat, dress, and have a place to sleep, and if you have a family, the burden is even greater. Many former inmates fight to go straight, but slowly find their way back to whatever got them in prison in the first place.

For me, parole was like a short rubber band that could snap me back into prison a million times faster than I had gotten out. My meager sense of being free on the outside vanished when my parole officer and probation officer, seeing me on Tuesdays and Thursdays, pounded into me that I was only out on parole, not free. *Like if I fart in the wrong part of town, sir, I'll find myself back in prison so fast it'll make my head spin.*

My parole officer would usually notify me when he was coming for a visit, but sometimes he would come around without notice. I wasn't breaking any laws, unless making love is a crime, but according to the rules and regulations of parole, I wasn't supposed to make love with anyone other than my legally wedded spouse. *They got to be kidding*!

One day I got real shook-up when my parole officer came

to visit and I was standing on the stoop talking to Bayamon, who had just gotten out of prison. I froze and whispered to Bayamon, "Diggit, here comes my parole officer," and Bayamon disappeared so smoothly and gracefully it was like he had vanished in a puff of smoke. If my parole officer recognized Bayamon as a parolee, he didn't let on. I figured he probably knew that most of the parolees came from neighborhoods like mine.

Yet try as hard as I could to cool my role, I couldn't help being nervous every time I reported or got visited. A parolee has no rights, and any bullshit complaint by a citizen can start him on his way back to prison. A parolee has got to walk on water because if he's picked up on his way home while something is happening on the street—a fight, somebody else pulling a job, or whatever—he is in for sweat's sake unless there is proof of innocence beyond a shadow of a doubt.

It was hard to deal with people who had never done time, especially when they knew I had. They would either clam up and look curiously at me or put on a big act of friendliness while also looking curiously at me. When I ran into an ex-con, it was like meeting a fraternity brother, even if I had hated his guts in prison.

It took me a long time before I was able to get the prison cockroaches out of my head. I'd wake up at home from nightmares that I was back in prison hearing the horrors, the curses and screams, reliving the tensions, anger, and pain, my body drenched in cold sweat. It would take minutes for me to realize I was at home.

When I first came home, I couldn't break the habit of waking up in the morning half-asleep, getting into my clothes and stumbling around my bedroom looking for the toilet bowl and wash bowl, then standing like a damn fool in front of my bedroom door waiting for the guard to spring the lock. While in prison, I had always fought against being institutionalized, but some of its habits had rubbed off on me a little too damn deep. Even now, twenty-four years later, I still have an occasional nightmare that I'm back in prison.

I've had occasion to visit prisons both here and in Puerto Rico, where I conducted group counseling for offenders who were in for drug-related crimes. Every time the gate shut behind me, a sense of horror stirred in me that the damn gate wouldn't open again. It may not show on my face, but the memories are burned deep inside me.

In prison, I had thought everything would be smooth sailing once I got out. Didn't I have a high-school equivalency diploma and a certificate in brick masonry stating that I had close to two thousand hours in the trade, stuccoing and laying cement blocks? I was going to be in clover with a well-paying job as a brick mason. First thing I found out was that I couldn't get past the union to work, and any non-union job was either digging holes or carrying bricks for someone who laid bricks as well as I did.

During the next few years, I worked in the garment district in New York City, part-time at Macy's Department store, as a salesman selling pots and pans door to door, as a baker for Fink Bakery, and in a foundry in Connecticut. It was a real struggle to make ends meet because these jobs didn't pay much, and I was fighting against the street pulling me back to making money the wrong way. I dropped the door-to-door salesman's job like a hot cake after I told my probation officer about it. He just stared at me and said, "Go ahead and sell door to door if you want. But if a housewife so much as complains you looked sideways at her, you've had it."

Soon after this, I began to work with street-gang kids in East Harlem and to write professionally, all the time with a certificate of brick masonry molding away in my bureau drawer. I became involved in making a film based on my work with the gang kids, and approached Mrs. Anna Kross, Commissioner of Corrections, for permission to film some sequences at Riker's Island. In the course of the conversation at her home, she said she had heard of the good work I was doing in the community. I told her I was interested in getting a job in her department in order to work with parolees and utilize my experience from both the streets and prison. Mrs.

Kross shook her head sadly and said, "I wish I could use your experience."

"So why not?" I pushed. "I'm willing and you seem to be."

Mrs. Kross again shook her head and said, "Impossible. First of all, with your prison record, you're not eligible to take a civil service exam, and even if you did, you'd be disqualified for the position because you don't have a degree."

I remember looking at her a long time before replying.

"Mrs. Kross, prison shouldn't be held against me no more than where I grew up. As for a degree, I have a doctorate in survival earned in two of the best schools in the country, the Harlem ghetto and prison."

"I understand what you are saying," she replied, "but my hands are tied."

Unfortunately, job discrimination against former convicts still exists today. In New York State, there is legislation that bars persons convicted of felonies from fifty or more jobs, including employment in bars, restaurants, liquor stores, banks, and insurance adjuster's offices, and also denies them the right to take certain civil service examinations and to engage in certain occupations licensed by the state, including doctor, lawyer, barber, junk-dealer, and others. There are legal procedures by which some of these employment barriers can be removed, and ex-offenders should be made aware of them.

Five years after my release from parole, I applied for and was granted a certificate of good conduct which restored my suffrage. Subsequently, I was called for jury duty and filled out a form that included the fact that I have been convicted of more than one felony. Upon reading my statement, the official was genuinely surprised, as if this were the first time a convicted felon had actually been called for jury duty. I have yet to hear from them.

I believe I have earned the full rights of citizenship. There are multitudes of us who have served our time but are still stigmatized by the label, "ex-offender." Society used to brand men and women on their foreheads to let the world know they were criminals. They don't use hot irons now, but the brand is still there. For its own dignity, as well as for the men and women who have paid their debt to society and for those inside prison walls, society must obliterate the stigma of "Once a con, always a con," and join in the acceptance of "Once a human, always a human."

APPENDIX 2

This list of organizations, publications, and special programs for former prisoners is by no means all-inclusive, but may serve as a basic resource.

ORGANIZATIONS

The following have local chapters across the country:

The American Civil Liberties Union (ACLU)
National Office
22 East 40 Street
New York, New York 10017

> *(The National Prison Project of the ACLU is at the New York State University at Buffalo Law School, 77 West Eagle, Buffalo, New York 14202.)*

American Friends Service Committee
National Office
160 North 15 Street
Philadelphia, Pennsylvania 19102

Community Action for Legal Services, Inc. (CALS)
335 Broadway
New York, New York 10013

> *(Legal Services Offices are found in every state.)*

NAACP Legal Defense Fund, Inc.
10 Columbus Circle
New York, New York 10019

National Lawyers Guild
23 Cornelia Street
New York, New York 10014

California

Black Law Journal Prisoners Program
Boalt Hall School of Law
Berkeley, California 94720

Coalition Against Repression
8162 Melrose Avenue
Los Angeles, California 90046

Committee United for Political Prisoners
701 West 34 Street
Los Angeles, California 90007

Elizabeth Fry Center
3429 West Olympic Boulevard
Los Angeles, California 90019

Prison Law Collective
558 Capp Street
San Francisco, California 94110

Prisoners' Union
1345 Seventh Avenue
San Francisco, California 94122

Project J.O.V.E. II
814 North Fair Oaks Avenue
Pasadena, California 91103

Women's Jail Project
588 Capp Street
San Francisco, California 94110

Connecticut

Connecticut Prison Association
340 Capital Avenue
Hartford, Connecticut 06115

Delaware

Community Legal Aid Society
204 West 7 Street
Wilmington, Delaware 19801

Delaware Council on Crime and Justice, Inc.
701 Shipley Street
Wilmington, Delaware 19801

District of Columbia

Board of Church and Society
United Methodist Church
Department of Law, Justice and Community Relations
100 Maryland Avenue N.E.
Washington, D.C. 20002

Bureau of Rehabilitation
412 5 Street N.W.
Washington, D.C. 20001

National Prisoners Alliance
2325 15 Street N.W.
Washington, D.C. 20036

Florida

Gainesville Legal Collective
115 South Main Street
Gainesville, Florida 32601

Georgia

Center for Correctional Reform
15 Peachtree Street, Suite 902
Atlanta, Georgia 30303

Legal Assistance to Inmates
Emory University School of Law
Atlanta, Georgia 30322

Prison Legal Group
P.O. Box 1932
Athens, Georgia 30601

Illinois

Cook County Special Bail Project
22 East Van Buren
Chicago, Illinois 60605

Medical Committee for Human Rights
2251 West Taylor Street
Chicago, Illinois 60612

People's Law Office
1215 West Sycamore
Carbondale, Illinois 62901

Prison Release Ministry, United Methodist Men
Northern Illinois Conference of the Methodist Church
1932 Lin-Lor Lane
Elgin, Illinois 60120

Radical Clearinghouse
Room 293, Illini Union
University of Illinois
Urbana, Illinois 61801

Kentucky

Southern Conference Educational Fund
3210 West Broadway
Louisville, Kentucky 40211

Maryland

Efforts from Ex-Convicts, Montgomery County
500 Gilscott Place
Rockville, Maryland 20850

The Prisoners Aid Association of Maryland
109 Old Town Bank Building
Gay Street at Fallsway
Baltimore, Maryland 21202

Massachusetts

Coalition to Fight Political Repression
P.O. Box 31
Cambridge, Massachusetts 02140

Prison Committee
8 Warren Street
Roxbury, Massachusetts 02119

Minnesota

Efforts from Ex-Convicts
2127 Riverside Avenue
Minneapolis, Minnesota 55404

Helping Industry Recruit Ex-Offenders (HIRE)
1931 Nicolett Avenue
Minneapolis, Minnesota 55403

Missouri
Citizens Lobby for Penal Reform
P.O. Box 13726
Kansas City, Missouri 64199

New York
Attica Defense Committee
P.O. Box 74, Bidwell Station
Buffalo, New York 14222

Center for Constitutional Rights
853 Broadway
New York, New York 10003

Fortune Society
29 East 22 Street
New York, New York 10010

National Committee for the Defense of Political Prisoners
P.O. Box 1184, Harlem Station
New York, New York 10027

National Conference of Black Lawyers
112 West 120 Street
New York, New York 10027

National Emergency Civil Liberties Committee
25 East 26 Street
New York, New York 10010

Women's Prison Association
110 Second Avenue
New York, New York 10003

Ohio

Concerned Convicts of America
1560 East 21 Street
Cleveland, Ohio 44114

Prisoner Support Group
Antioch College
Yellow Springs, Ohio 45387

The Seven Steps Foundation
133 East Market Street
Akron, Ohio 44308

Oregon

National Prisoners' Alliance
215 Southeast 9 Street
Portland, Oregon 97214

Pennsylvania

Community Release Agency
1100 Lawyers Building
Pittsburgh, Pennsylvania 15203

Imprisoned Citizens Union
P.O. Box 4731
Philadelphia, Pennsylvania 19134

Pennsylvania Program for Women and Girl Offenders
1530 Chestnut Street, Suite 711
Philadelphia, Pennsylvania 19102

People's Bail Fund
1411 Walnut Street, Suite 1201
Philadelphia, Pennsylvania 19102

Prisoners' Rights Council
1 North 13 Street
Philadelphia, Pennsylvania 19107

Virginia
Penal Reform Institute
P.O. Box 234
110 North Royal Street
Alexandria, Virginia 22313

Washington
Administration of Criminal Justice and Prison Reform
    Committee
Young Lawyers Section of the ABA
Prison Law Reporter
Hoge Building, 15th Floor
Seattle, Washington 98105

Inside-Out
106 21 Street East
Seattle, Washington 98105

Wisconsin
Correctional Service Federation
526 West Wisconsin Avenue
Milwaukee, Wisconsin 53203

PUBLICATIONS

Civil Liberties Review
22 East 40 Street
New York, New York 10016

Committee for Prison Humanity & Justice Newsletter
1029 4 Street
San Rafael, California 94901

*Directory of Services and Programs for Former Prisoners
    in New York State*
Action Council of the New York Urban Coalition
55 Fifth Avenue
New York, New York 10003

Fortune News
29 East 22 Street
New York, New York 10010

How to Regain Your Rights
Action Council of the New York Urban Coalition
55 Fifth Avenue
New York, New York 10003

Midnight Special
23 Cornelia Street
New York, New York 10014

Prisoners' Digest International
P.O. Box 89
Iowa City, Iowa 52240

Southern Patriot
c/o SCEF
3210 West Broadway
Louisville, Kentucky 40211

The Outlaw
1345 Seventh Avenue
San Francisco, California 94122

SPECIAL PROGRAMS

Development and Training Center for the Distributive
Trades, Inc.
District 65, Distributive Workers of America
13 Astor Place
New York, New York 10003

*Funded by the Manpower and Career Development
Agency (MCDA) of the Human Resources
Administration, City of New York*

*Comprehensive program of job training, counseling
and follow-up.*

Manhood Foundation, Inc.
512 West 125 Street, New York, New York 14226
1910 Arthur Avenue, Bronx, New York 10451
270 Flatbush Avenue, Brooklyn, New York 11226
89-30 161 Street, Jamaica, New York 11431

*Funded by MCDA. Job development, training, and
placement, Drug abuse program.*

Opportunities Industrialization Centers, Inc.
1024 Fulton Street, Brooklyn, New York 11201
1260 Boston Post Road, Bronx, New York 10451
444 Lenox Avenue, New York, New York 14226
614 East 14 Street, New York, New York 10003

*Funded by Office of Economic Opportunity, Human
Resources Administration, and Private Sources.*

*Job training in refrigeration services, food services,
secretarial skills, IBM key punch, etc. Comprehensive
support services.*

Project Rebound (NAACP)
2521 Broadway
New York, New York 10025

> *Provides personal counseling for job placement, as
> well as referrals to other agencies for education,
> training, etc.*

VERA Institute for Criminal Justice
Public Sector Job Development
30 East 39 Street
New York, New York 10016

> *Salaried jobs in public projects, such as newspaper
> recycling, sidewalk repair, and water blasting.*

GLOSSARY

aguacates: alligator pears
alma: soul
amigo: friend
antip tico, un: a non-sympa-
  thizer
arroz con pollo: chicken and
  rice
asco: disgust
ay: alas

baño: bathtub
belleza: beauty
bien: well
blanco: white, "whitey"
blanco-americano: white
  American
blanquitos: "whitey,"
  "honkies"
bris: "buddy-o"
buena suerte: good luck

caramba: "hot damn"
casa: home
chévere: great
chica: little girl, "baby"
chota: "squealer," "rat,"
  "fink"
compadre: pal, old buddy

coño: cunt
coquís: singing Puerto Rican
  tree frogs
coquito: Puerto Rican egg-
  nog made of white rum,
  coconut milk, eggs, and
  sugar
corazón: heart
cuerpo: body
culo: ass, tail

de nada: you're welcome, it's
  nothing

¿Entiendes?: Understand?

familia, la: the family
finca: farm
feliz cumpleaños: happy
  birthday
"Flaco": "Skinny"
frutas: fruits

Gloria de Dios, La: Heaven,
  God's glory
gracias: thanks

hermano: brother

Seven Long Times

hijo: son
hijo de la gran puta: son of the big whore
hola: hello
hombre: man

lechón asado: roast pork
limpio: clean

mañana: tomorrow
maricón: faggot, queer
mejor: better
mi madre: my mother
mierda: shit
muchacha: girl
mucho: much, a lot, very
muchos están contigo: many are with you
muchos ricos: many rich people
muerto: dead
mujeres: women

nada: nothing
no te apures: don't worry
numero: number
nunca: never

¡Oye!: Hey, listen!

pajaritos: little birds
palabra: word
panín: buddy
panita: buddy, partner
papo: "daddy-o"
pavo: turkey
pendejo: pubic hair, "asshole"

pistolas: pistols
por Dios: by God, for God's sake
por favor: please
¿Por qué?: Why?
¿Por qué no?: Why not?
presidio, el: the prison
puro corazón: pure heart

¡Qué mierda!: What shit!

salsa: sauce, "Latin rhythm"

tecato: junkie
Tía: Aunt
todo bien: very well
¿Tu qué?: You what?
tu también: you, too

viva: hurrah

yerba: herb, grass, "pot"